OUIJA ANSWER BOOK

LOOK INTO THE FUTURE.
HAVE FUN!

STERLING INNOVATION
An imprint of Sterling Publishing Co., Inc.

New York / London
www.sterlingpublishing.com

STERLING, the Sterling logo, STERLING INNOVATION, and the Sterling Innovation logo are registered trademarks of Sterling Publishing Co., Inc.

2 4 6 8 10 9 7 5 3 1

Published by Sterling Publishing Co., Inc.
387 Park Avenue South, New York, NY 10016

Distributed in Canada by Sterling Publishing
c/o Canadian Manda Group, 165 Dufferin Street
Toronto, Ontario, Canada M6K 3H6
Distributed in the United Kingdom by GMC Distribution Services
Castle Place, 166 High Street, Lewes, East Sussex, England BN7 1XU
Distributed in Australia by Capricorn Link (Australia) Pty. Ltd.
P.O. Box 704, Windsor, NSW 2756, Australia

Design by StarGraphics Studio

Printed in China

Sterling ISBN 978-1-4027-6747-0

For information about custom editions, special sales, premium and corporate purchases, please contact Sterling Special Sales Department at 800-805-5489 or specialsales@sterlingpublishing.com.

INTRODUCTION

Life is a journey both wonderful and mysterious. We look for answers to its greatest questions in the tomes of spirituality and philosophy. But sometimes the answers lie within ourselves; in dreams and the unconscious mind. We are only in need of a medium to interpret the complex workings of our minds—to get at our true hopes, fears, and desires.

This book, like the traditional Ouija Board, will act as a bridge between the unconscious and consciousness mind, putting questioners in touch with their true nature and guiding them on a path best suited to them. By delving deep into the self and allowing the unconscious mind to surface, questioners are able to find genuine answers that will bring joy and contentment into their lives.

Because the nature of the mind is so complex, you may have to think intensively about the answers you are given. Sometimes they will be unexpected, or maybe they will not make sense at first. But by focusing with an open mind on a question, and putting all preconceived answers aside, this book can explain your dreams and spell out your true destiny. The answers may surprise you!

INSTRUCTIONS

The Ouija Answer Book is a personal, portable medium for answering all your questions. The only other things you need are a pen, some paper, and an open mind.

1. Begin by focusing on a question. You can ask anything you want, from what a troubling dream meant to whether you should take a job you were offered. Clear your mind of everything except for your question. Do your best to put aside any preconceptions you may have.

2. Flip randomly to anywhere in the entire book. There are a variety of ways in which it can provide you with your answer:

   - You may get an answer right away in the form of a Yes or a No.

   - You may find a letter on each page. Write both letters down and continue flipping. Once you feel satisfied with your list of letters, begin trying to find words in it. For example, if you have O/P, A/B, T/U, G/I, E/F, M/N, B/C, and E/F written down, then PATIENCE may be the answer to your question. There is no

exact science of the mind or of Ouija, so there may be a letter or two that is unnecessary and may be discarded in the spelling of your final answer. Don't be hasty though—be sure to consider all possible meanings. If your set of letters doesn't seem to make sense, you may want to try asking the question again.

- You may also find numbers on the pages you flip to. Write down the numbers the same way you did the letters, and look for your answer there. Number answers can be more cryptic than letter answers, so do your best to think critically about the numbers you are given. They may be someone's birthday, an address, or a phone number that will lead you to your answer.

- If you flip to Good Bye, you are not truly ready to have this question answered. Consider asking a different question, perhaps one that will prepare you for your original question.

- It is likely that you will come up with a combination of the different answer types. Sometimes your answer will be obvious, but other times—usually for more complex questions—you may have to look below the surface to interpret the correct answers. Always remember to keep an open mind and have fun!

YES

A

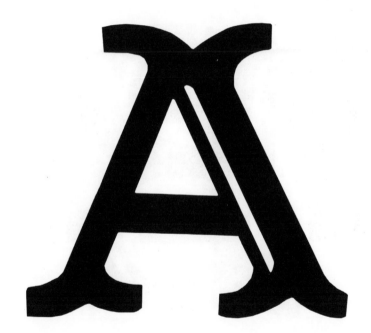

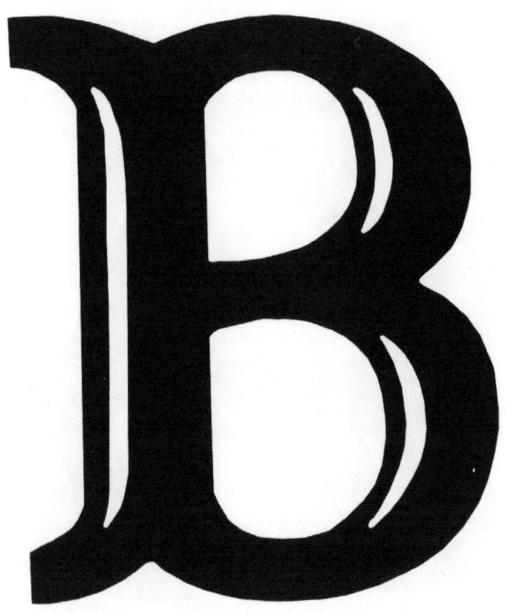

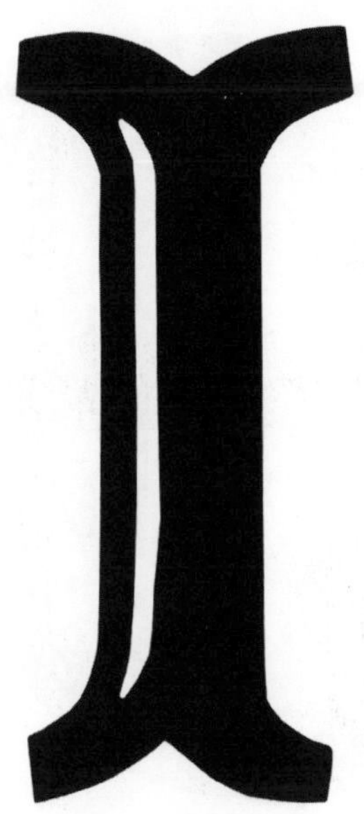

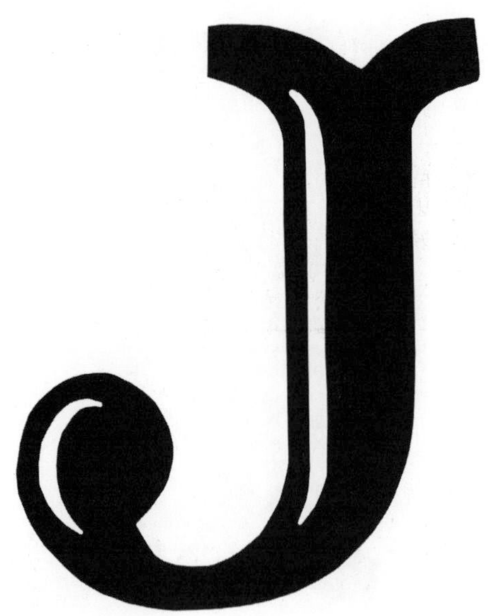

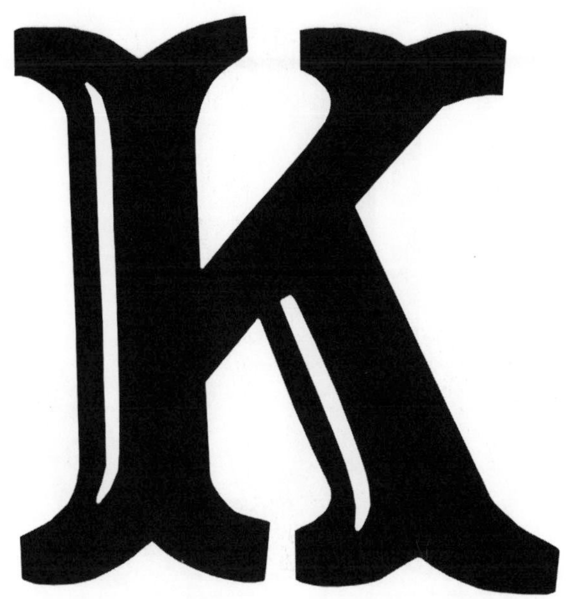

M

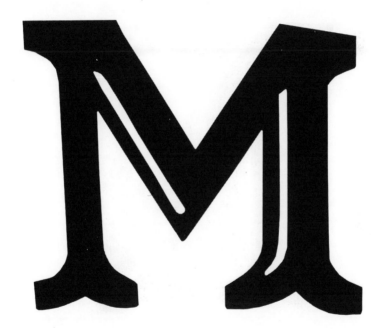

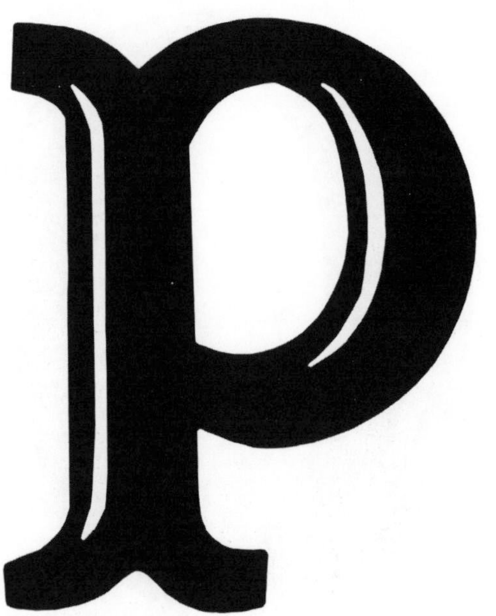

Q

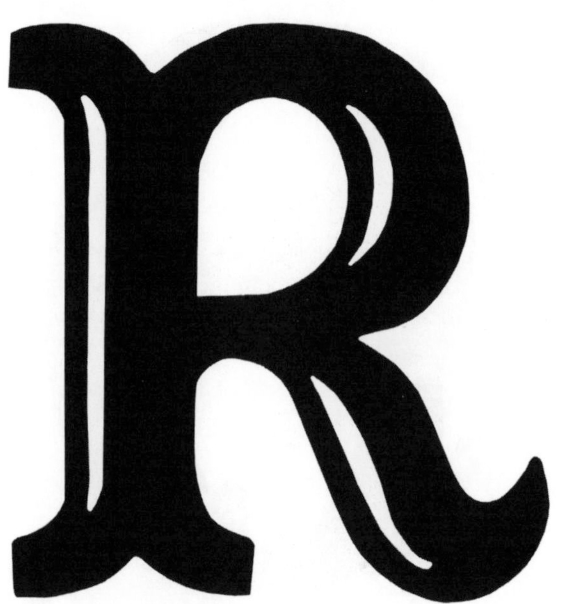

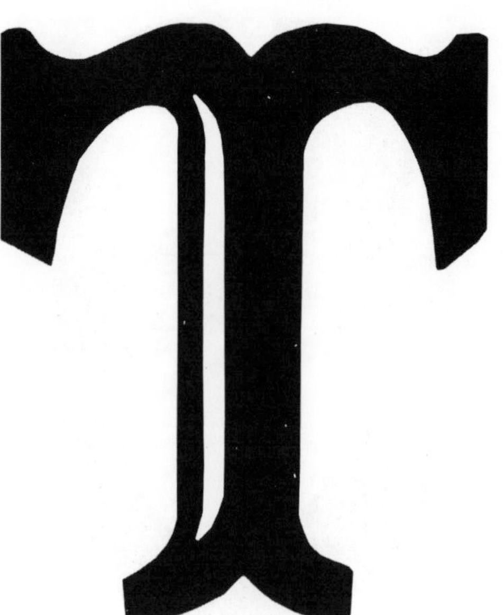

W

Y

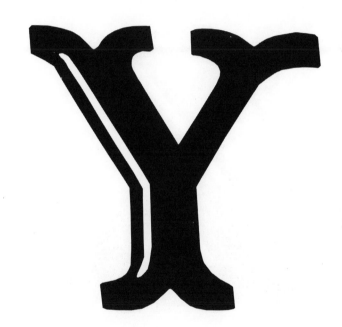

NO

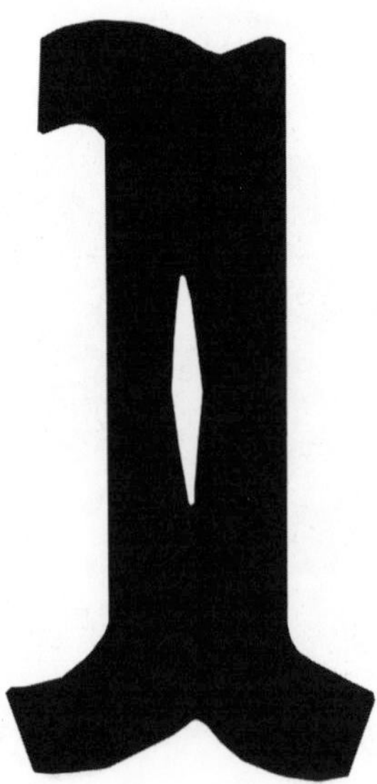

5

GOOD BYE

YES

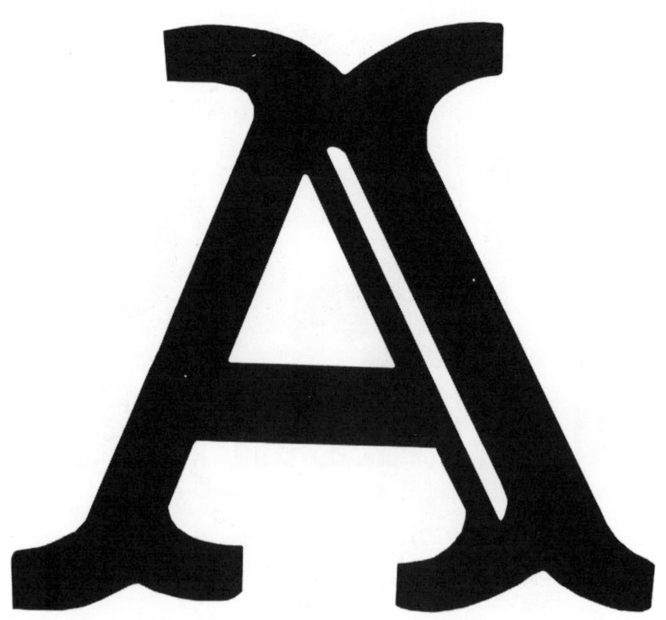

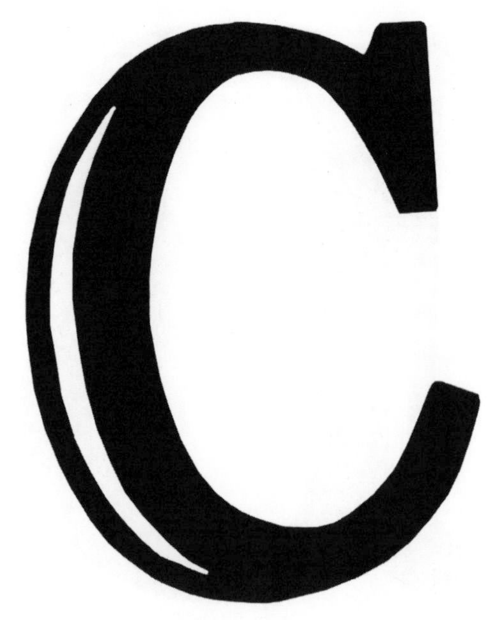

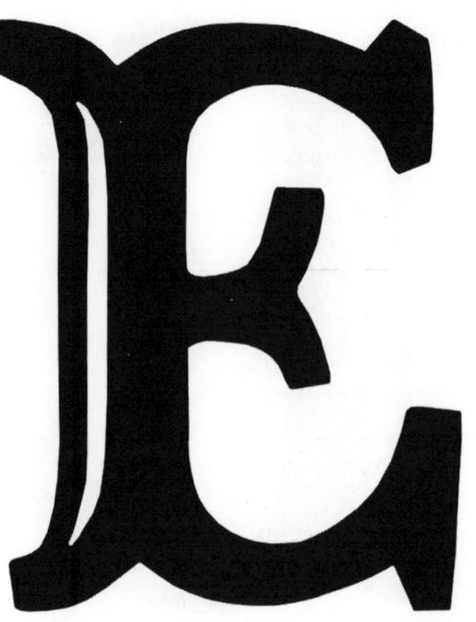

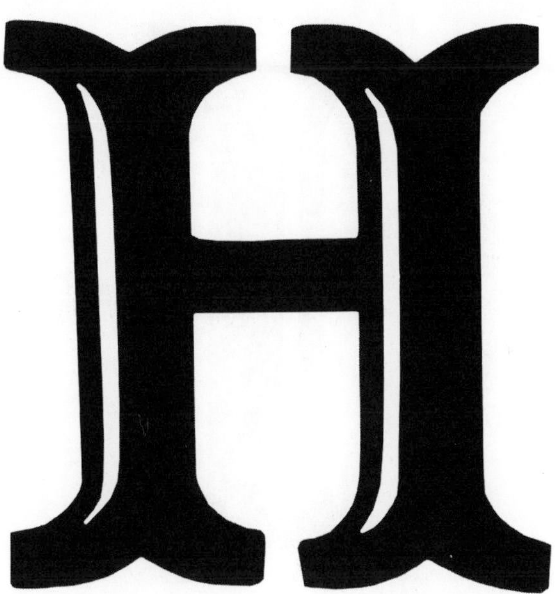

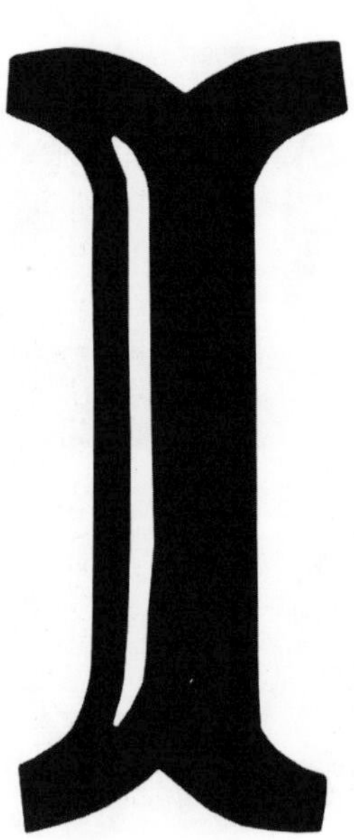

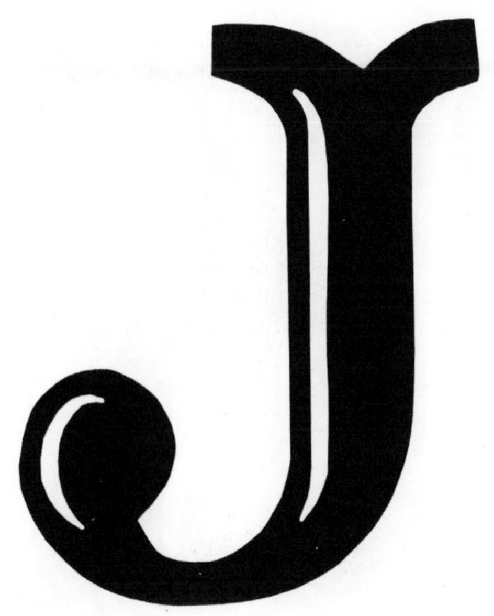

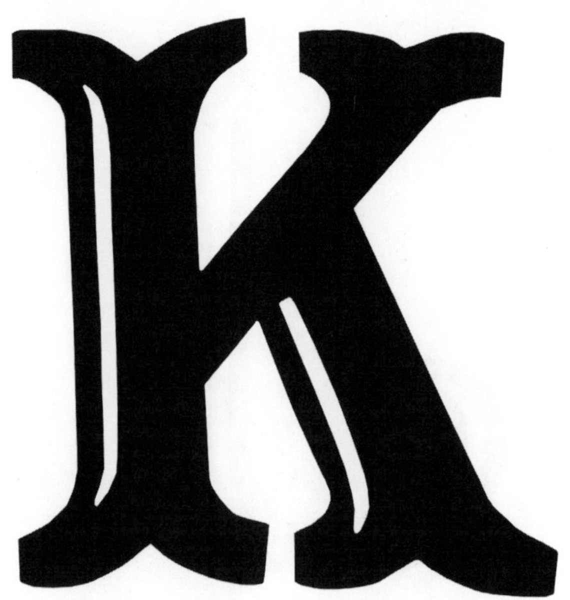

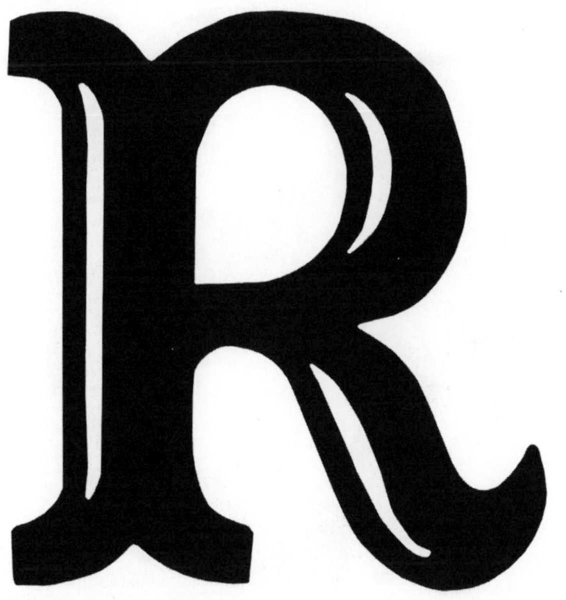

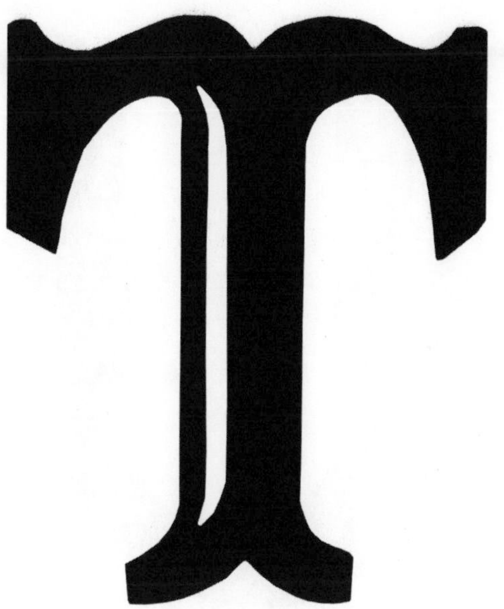

W

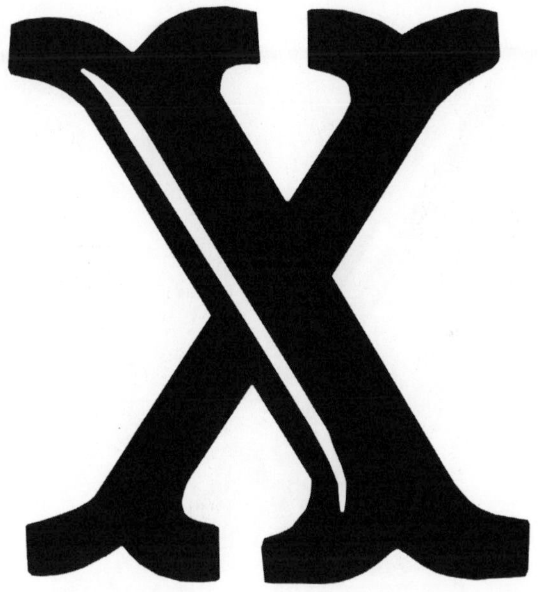

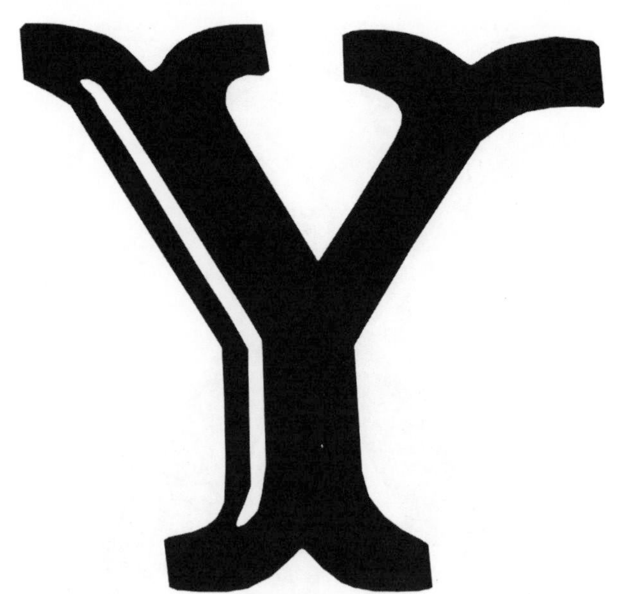

NO

GOOD BYE

YES

A

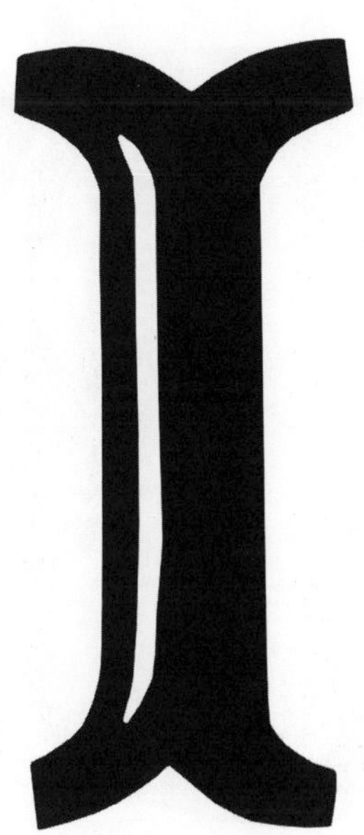

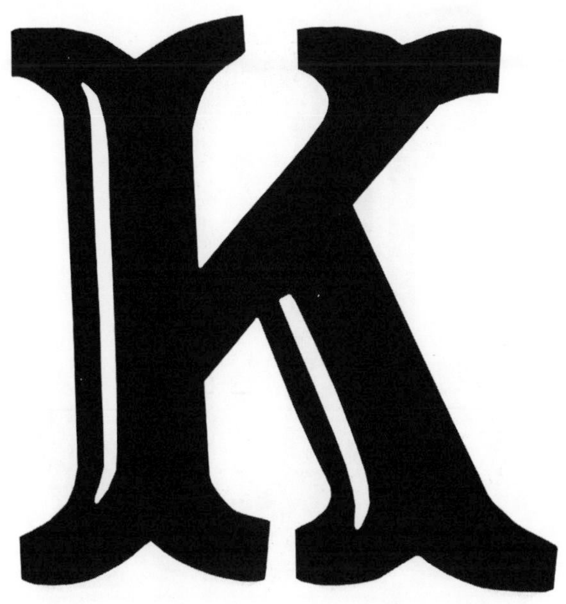

M

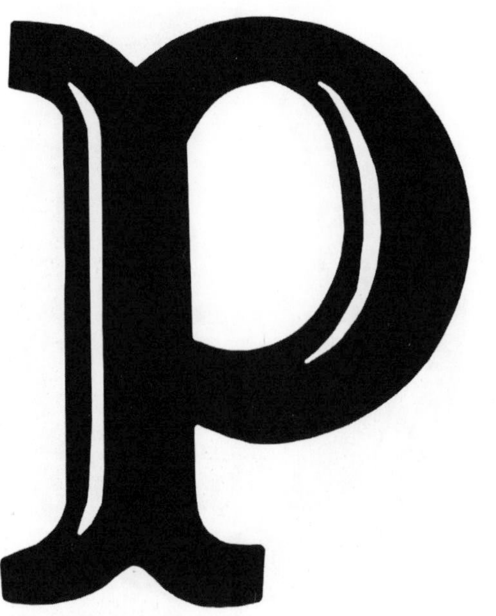

Q

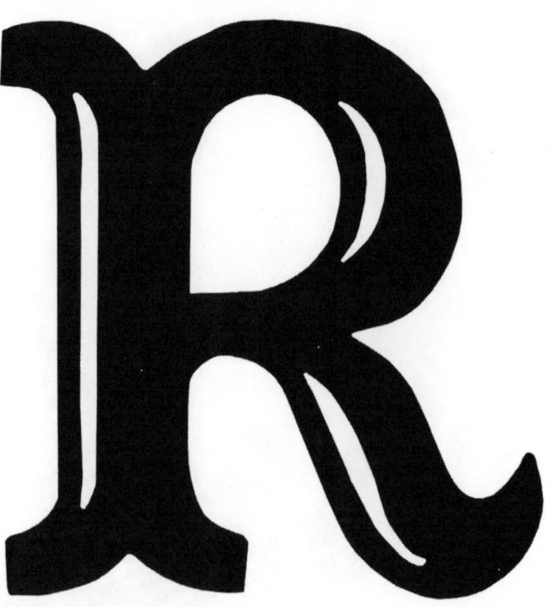

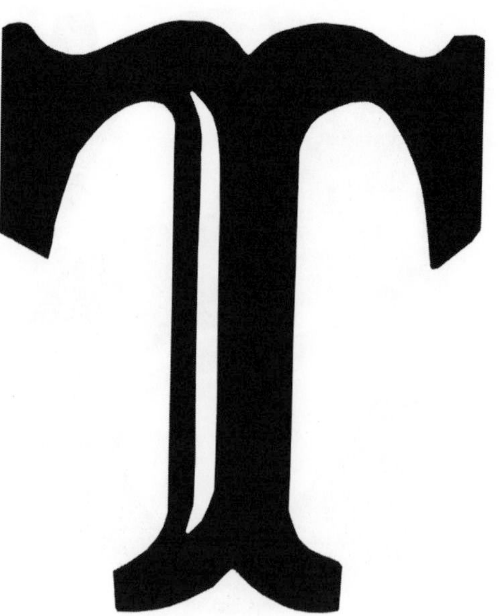

W

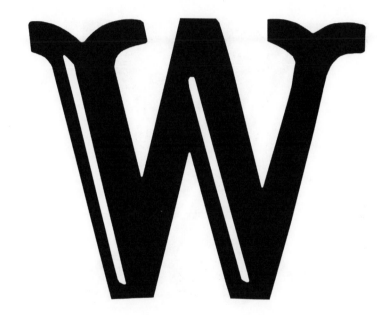

Y

NO

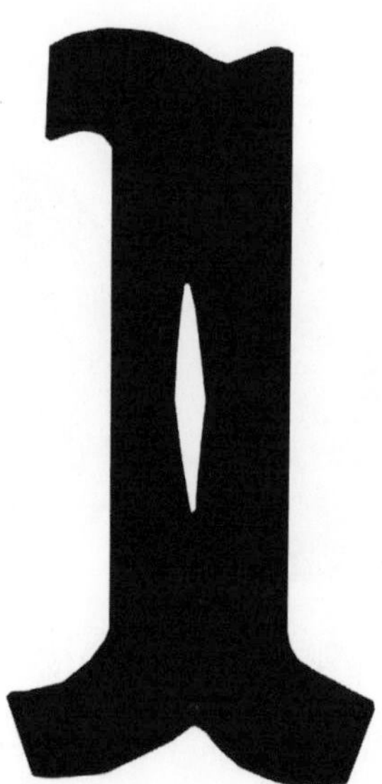

5

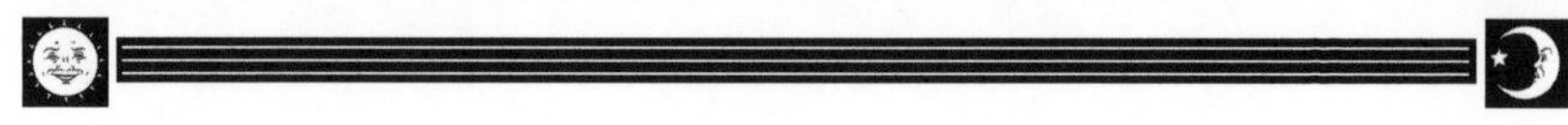

GOOD BYE

YES

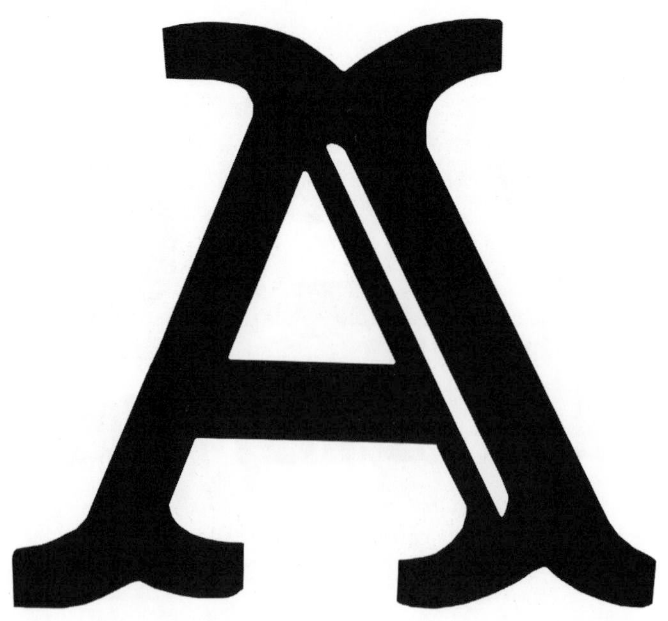

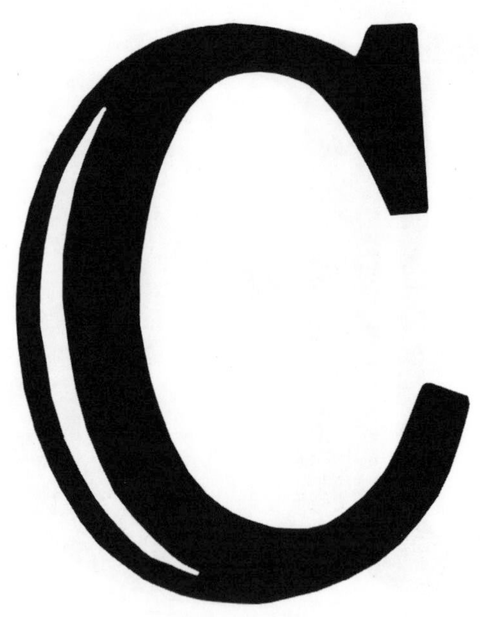

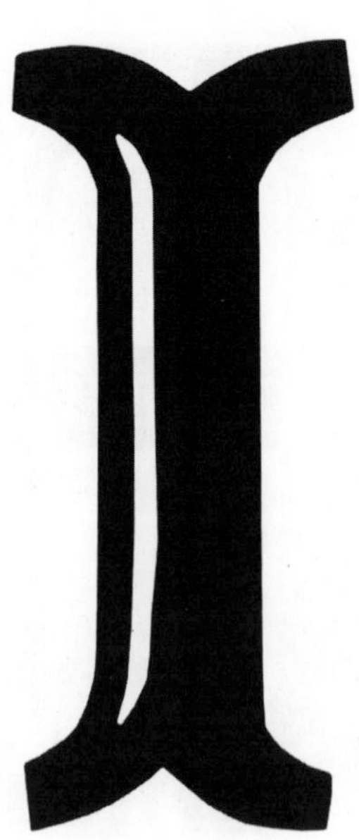

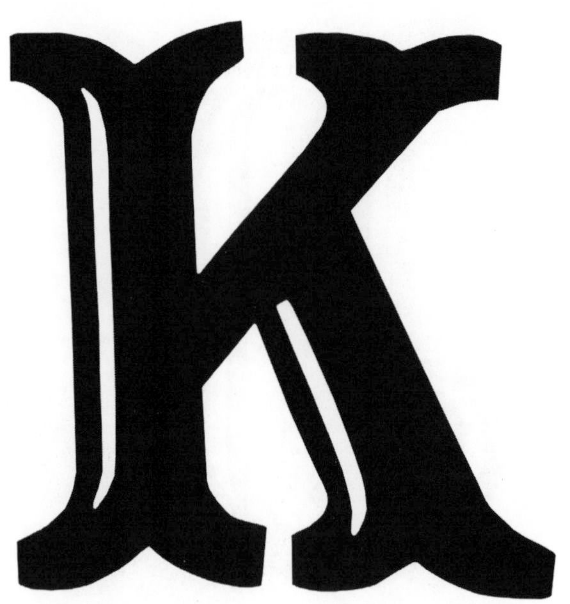

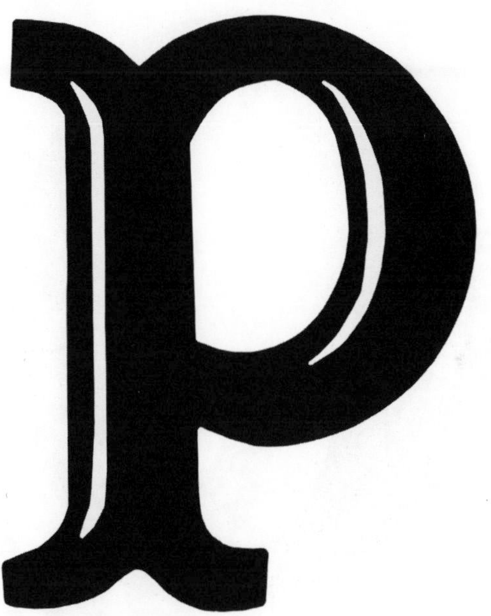

Q

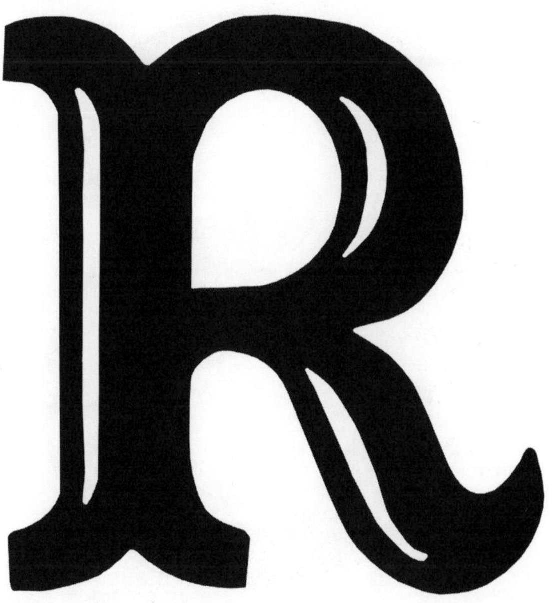

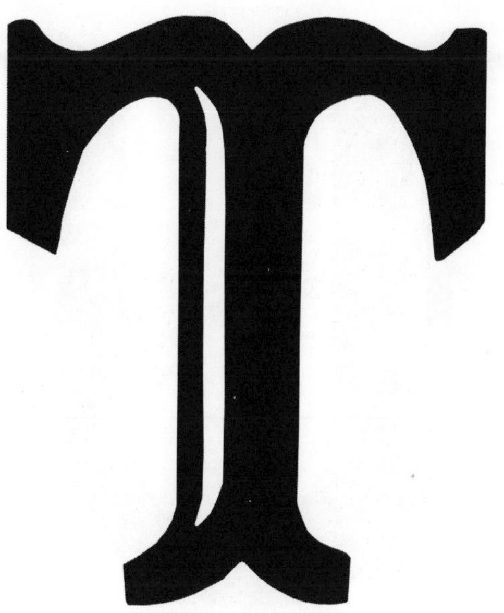

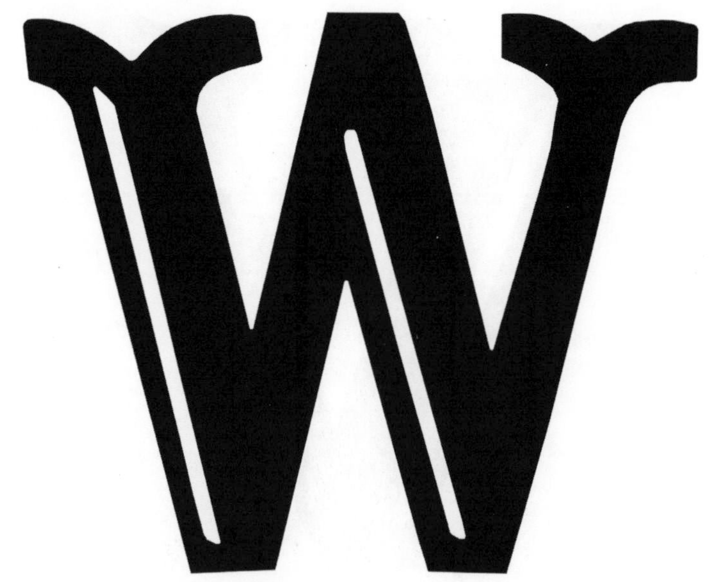

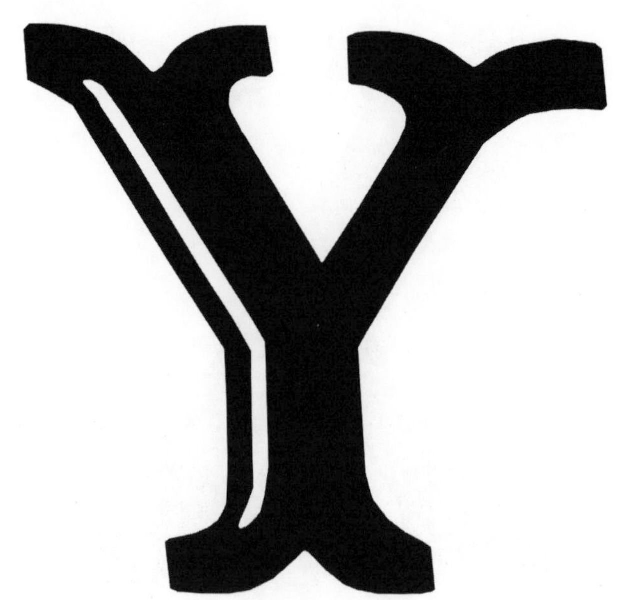

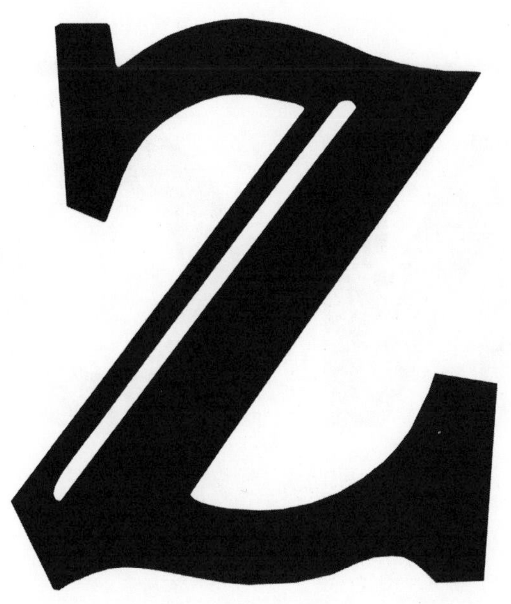

NO

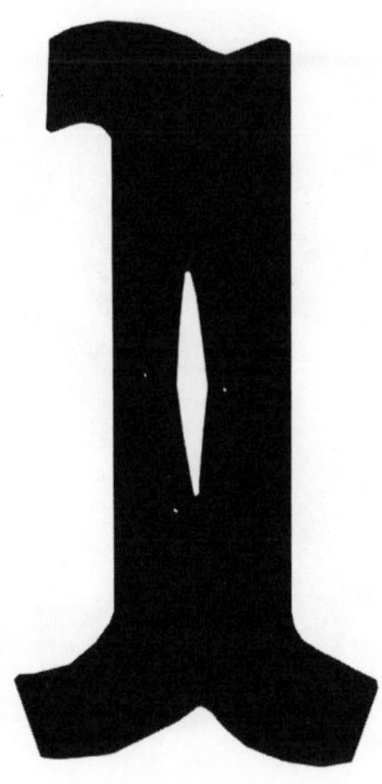

5

GOOD BYE

YES

A

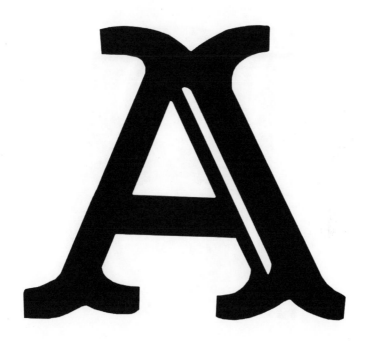

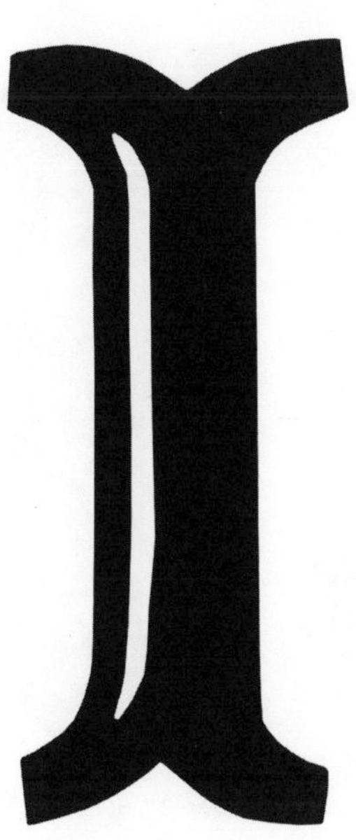

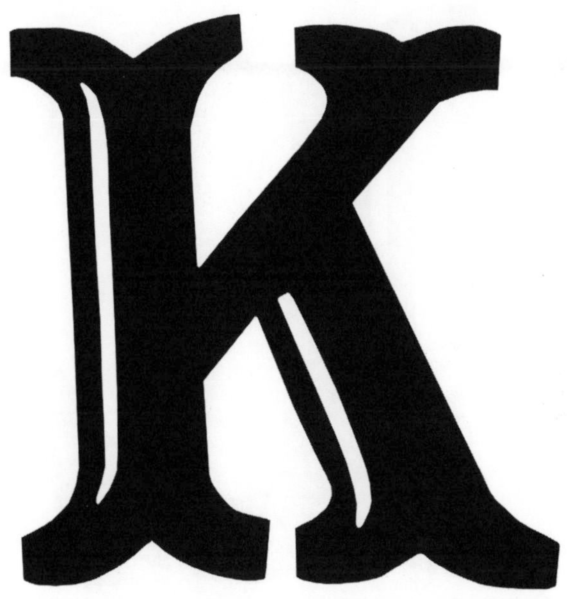

M

Q

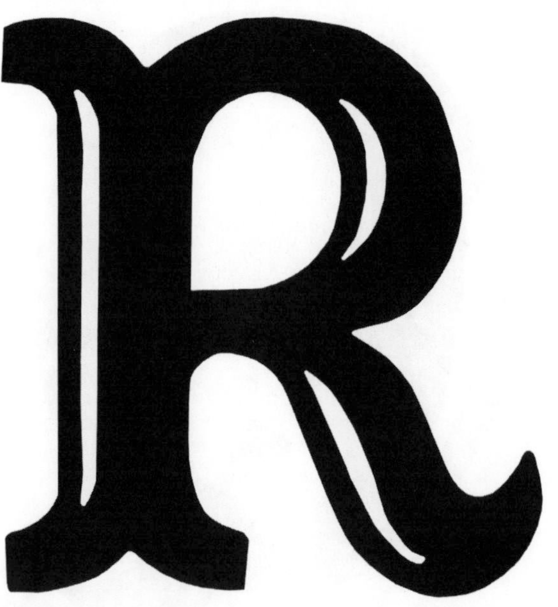

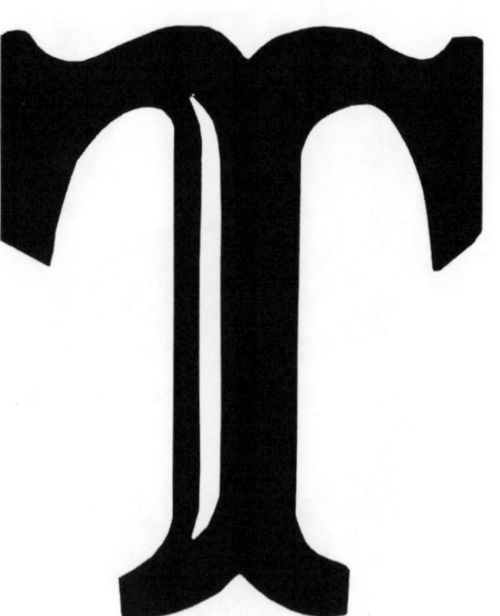

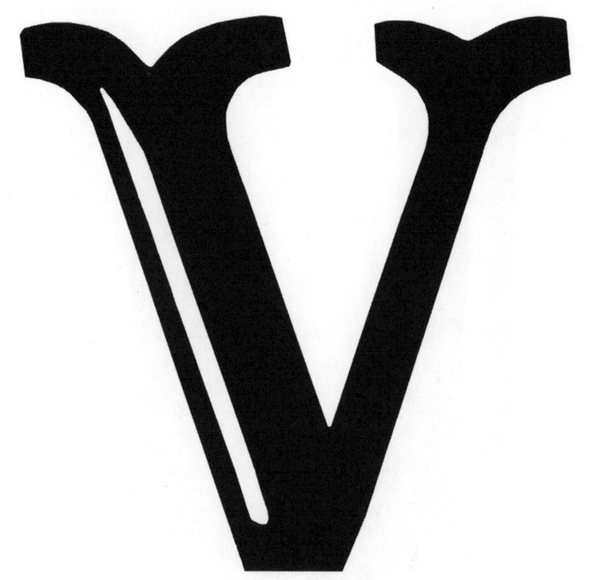

W

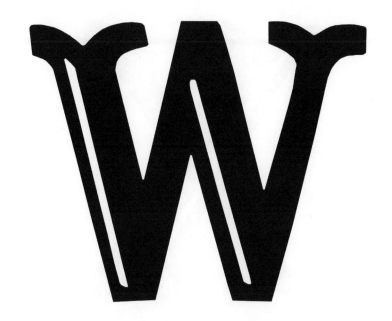

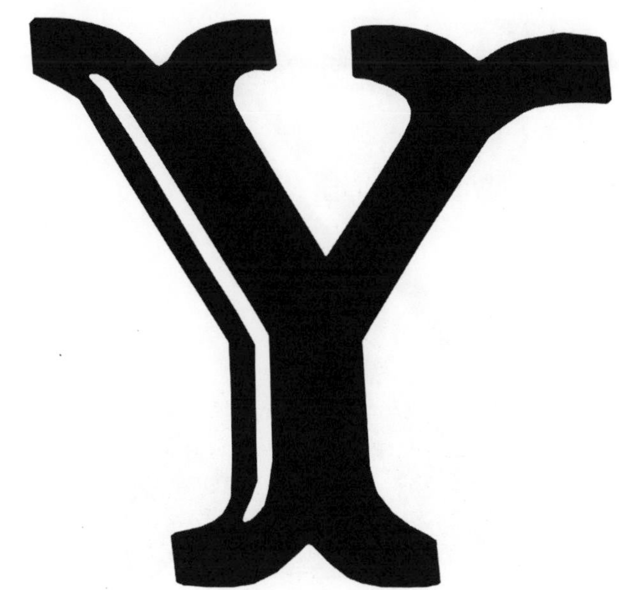

NO

5

GOOD BYE

YES

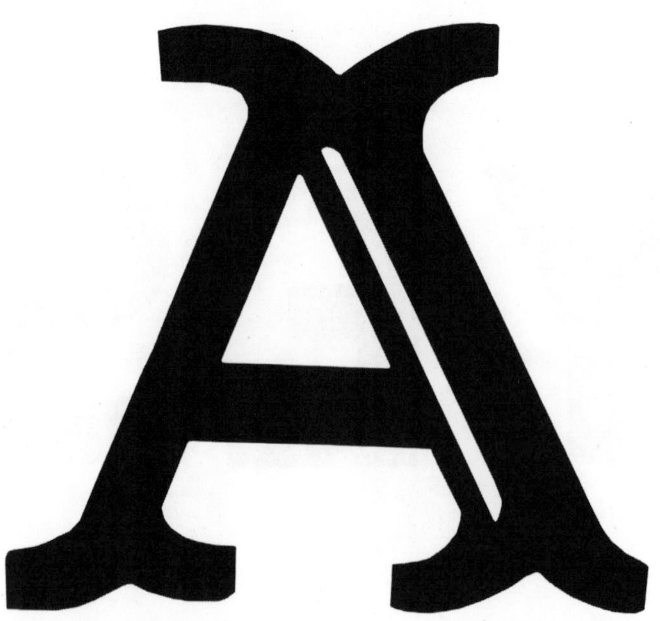

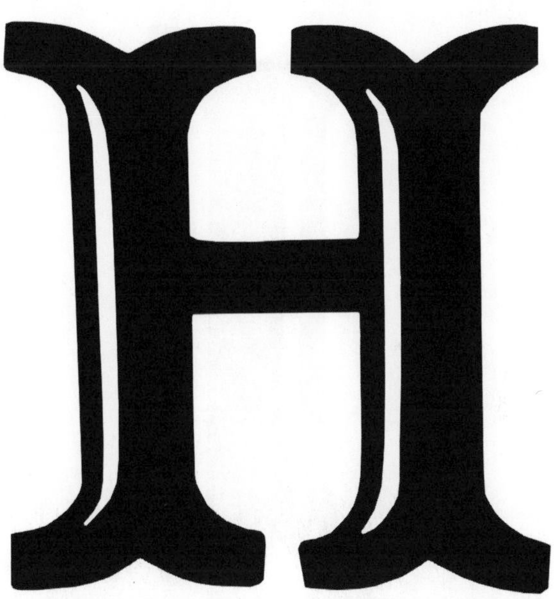

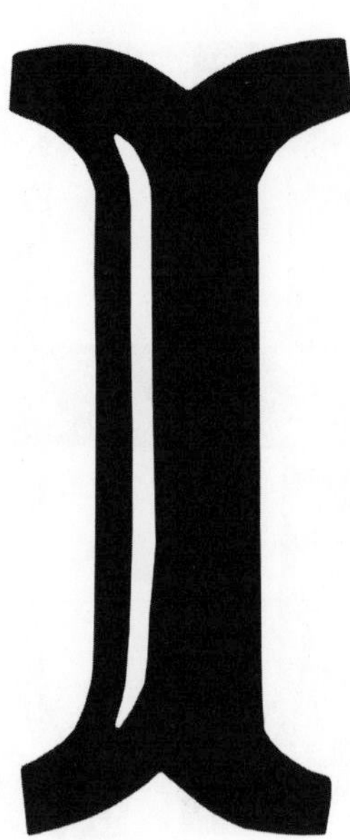

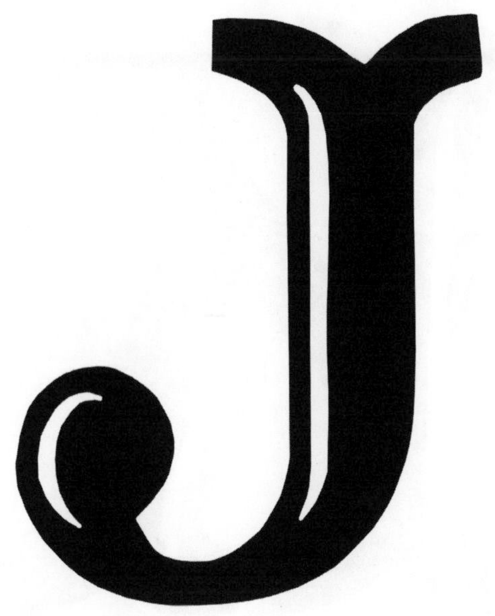

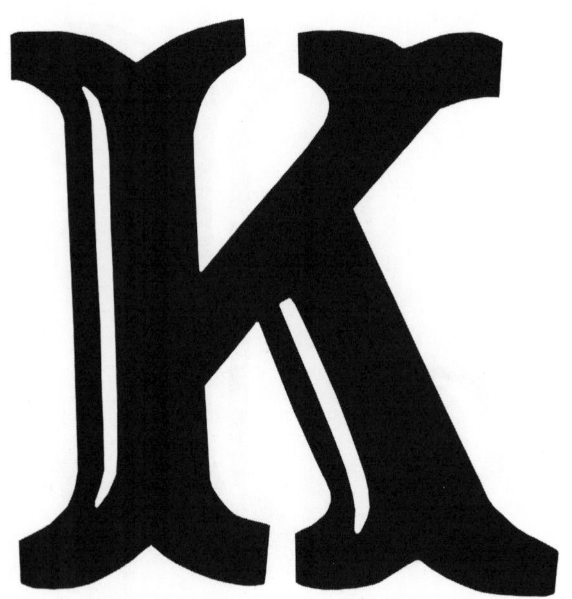

Q

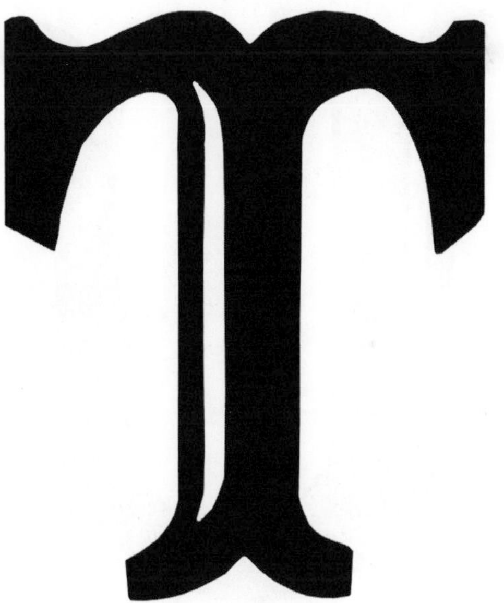

W

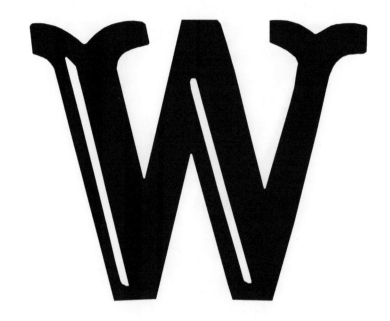

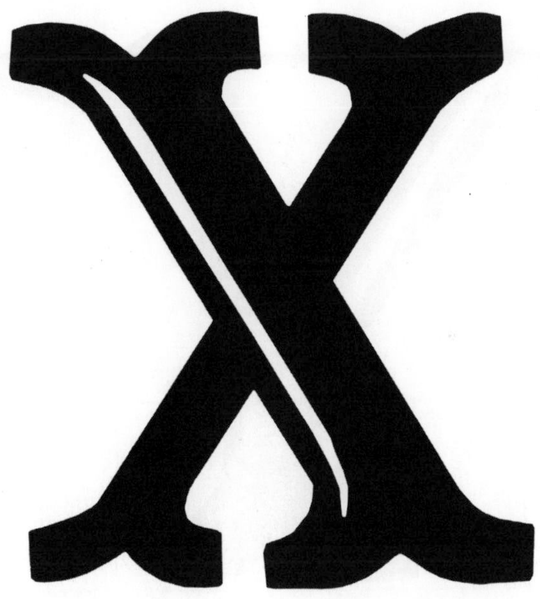

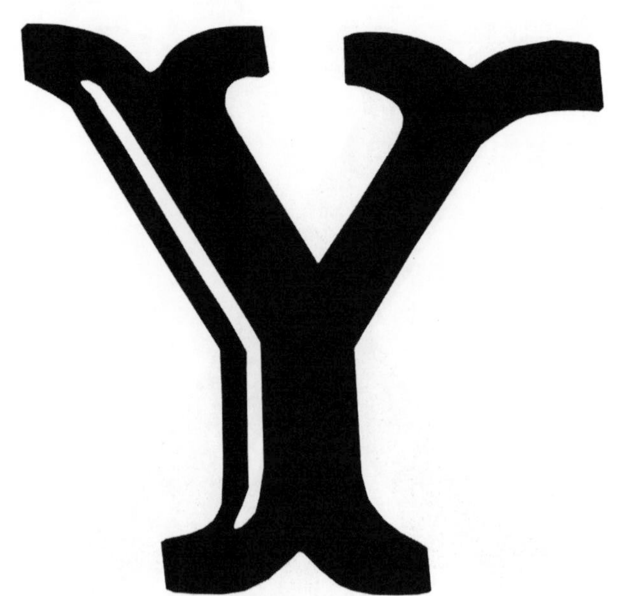

NO

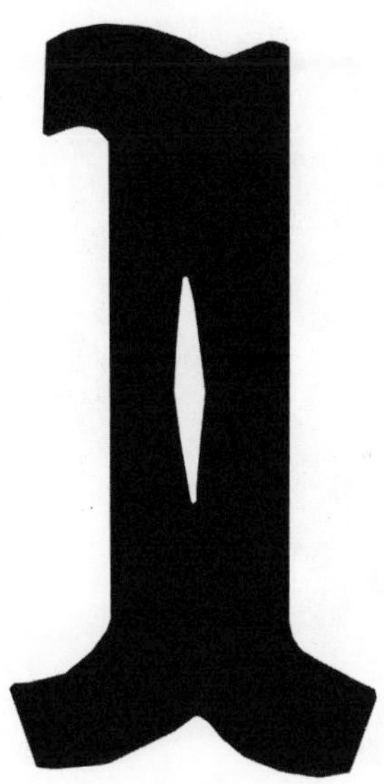

5

GOOD BYE

YES

A

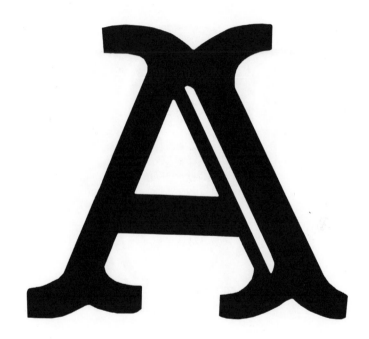

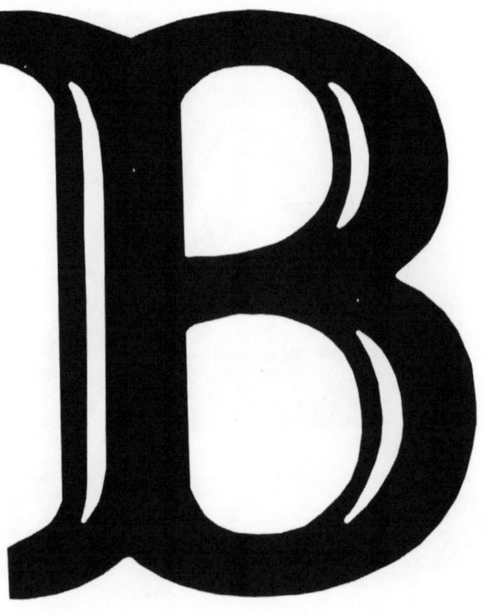

H

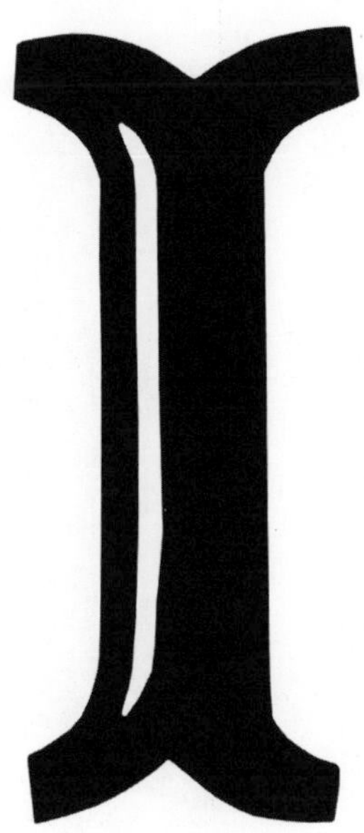

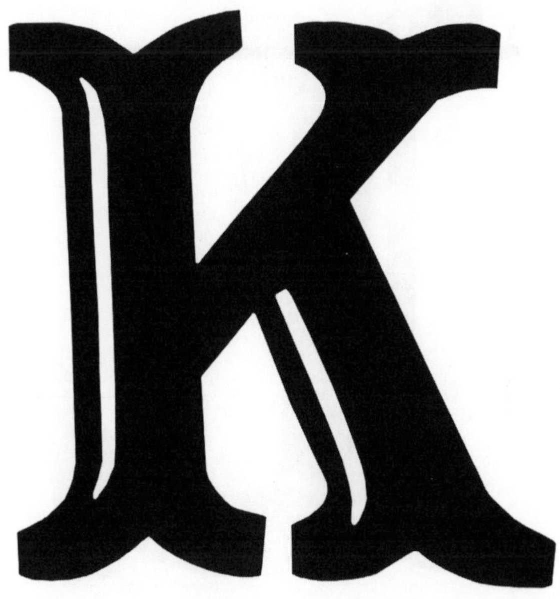

M

Q

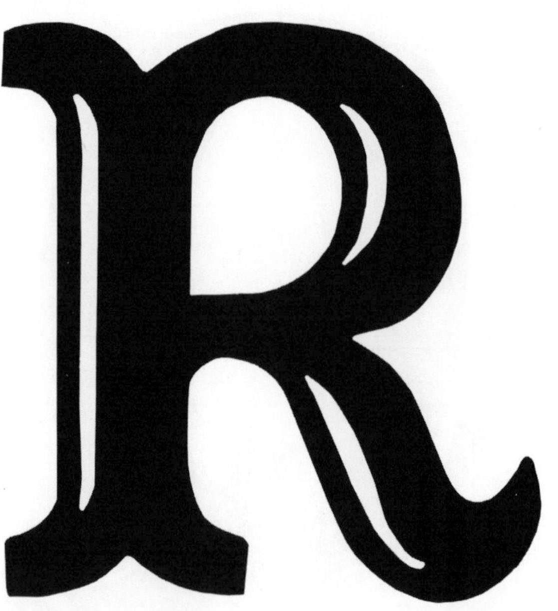

W

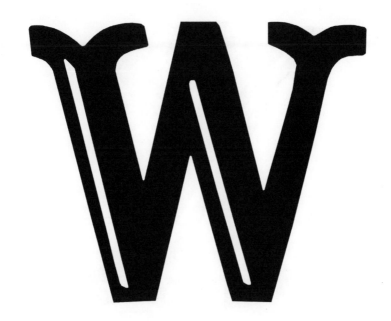

Y

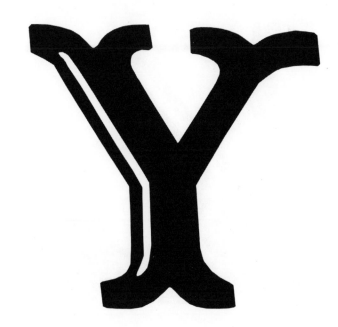

NO

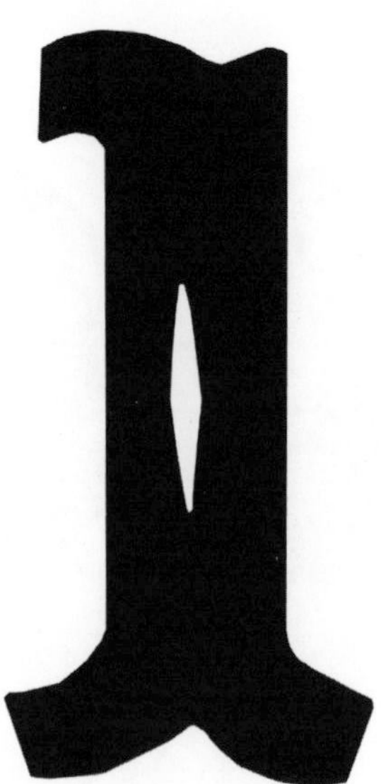

5

GOOD BYE

YES

A

H

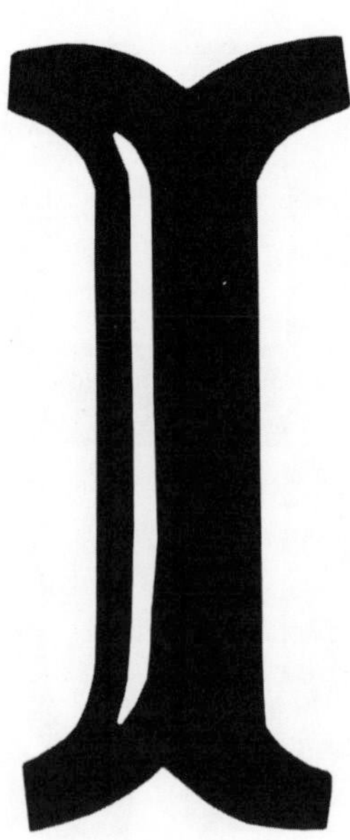

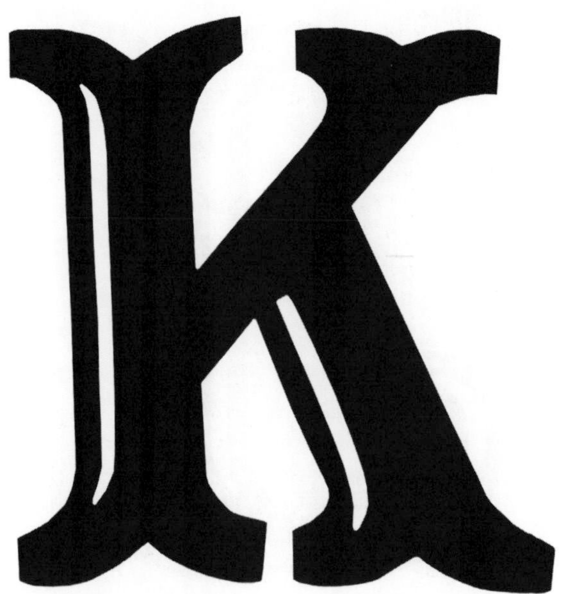

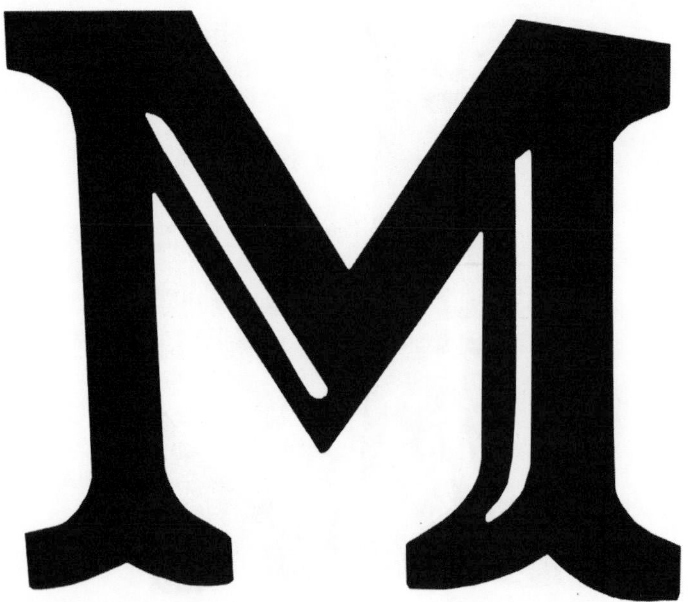

Q

W

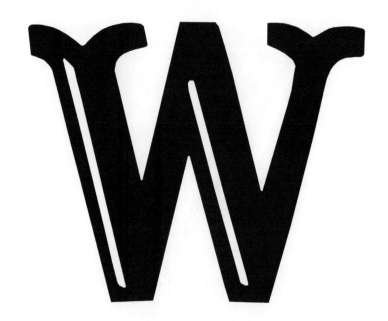

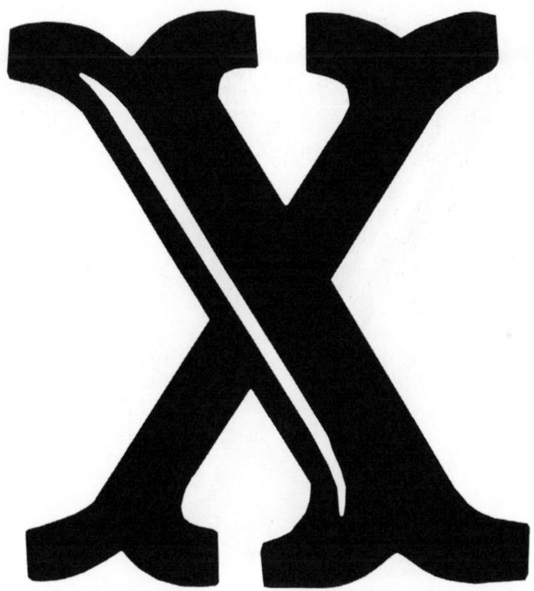

Y

NO

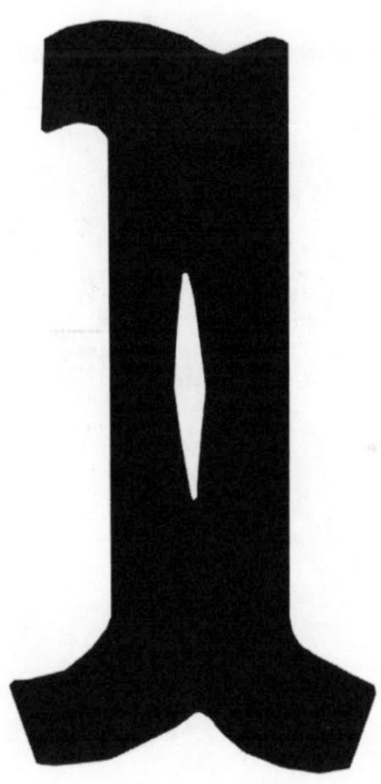

3

5

GOOD BYE

YES

A

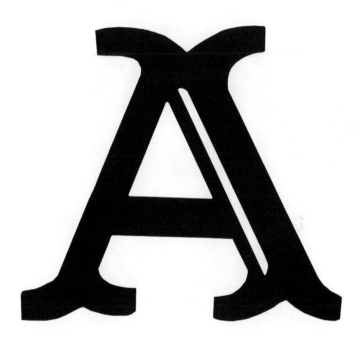

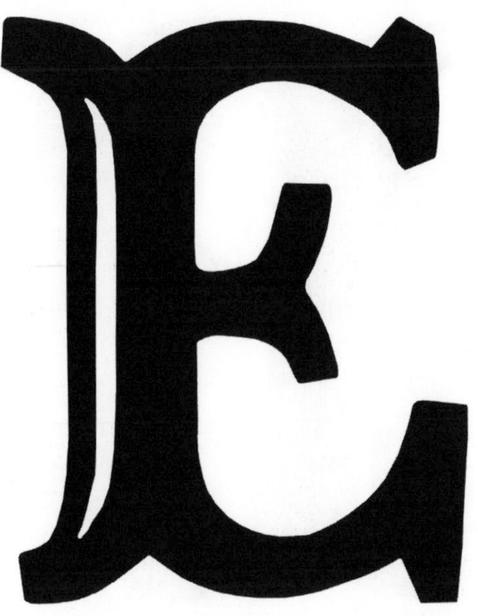

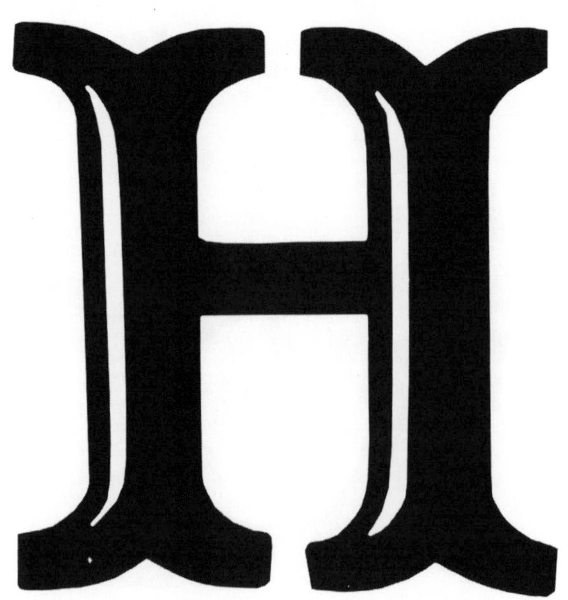

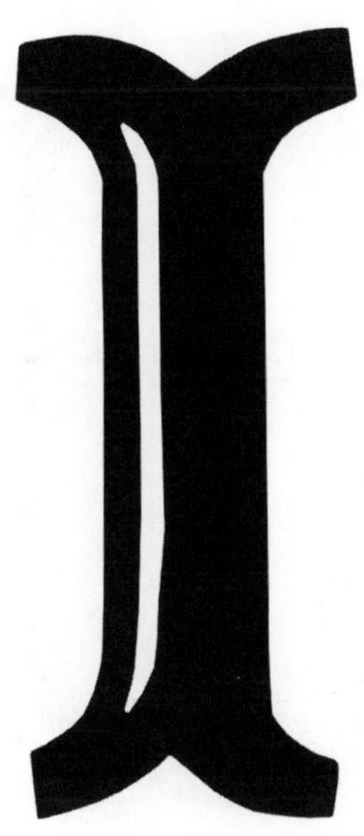

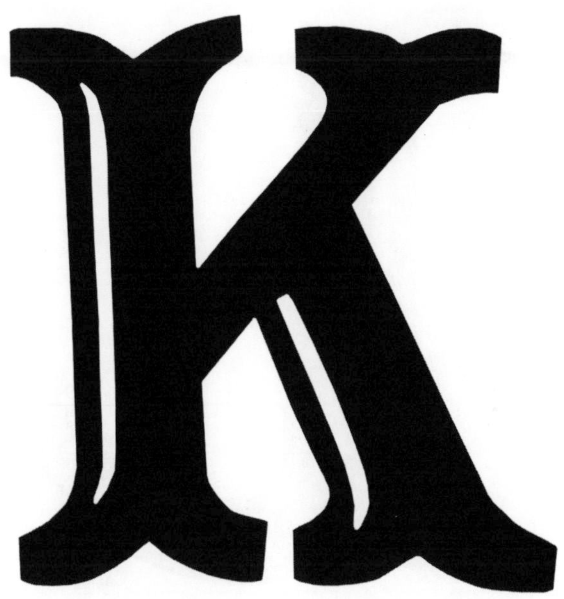

M

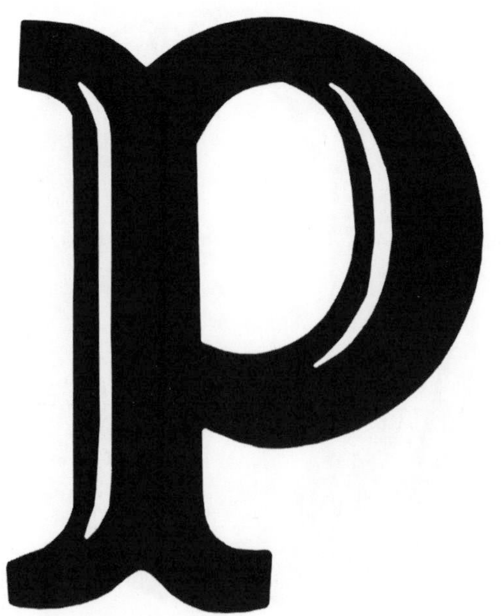

Q

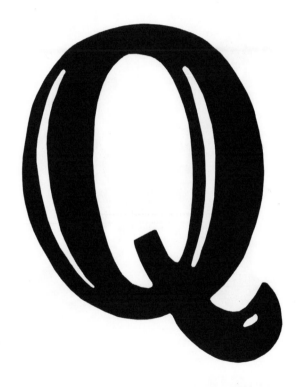

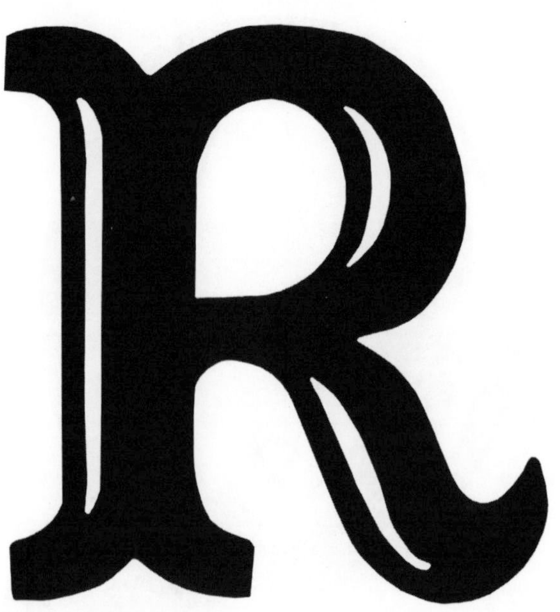

W

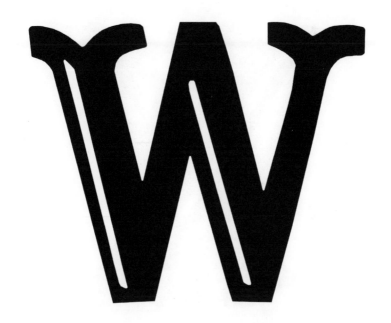

Y

NO

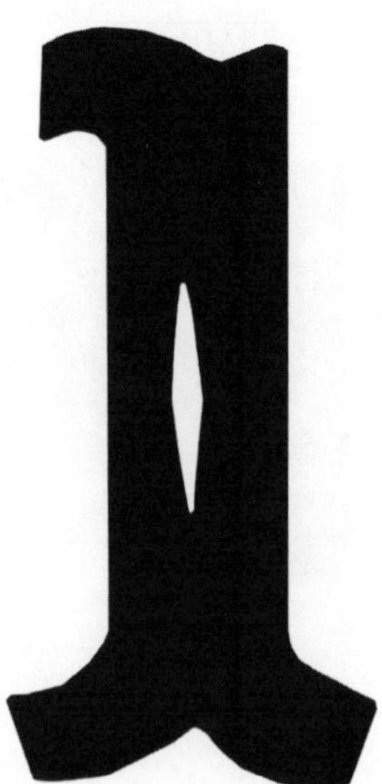

3

5

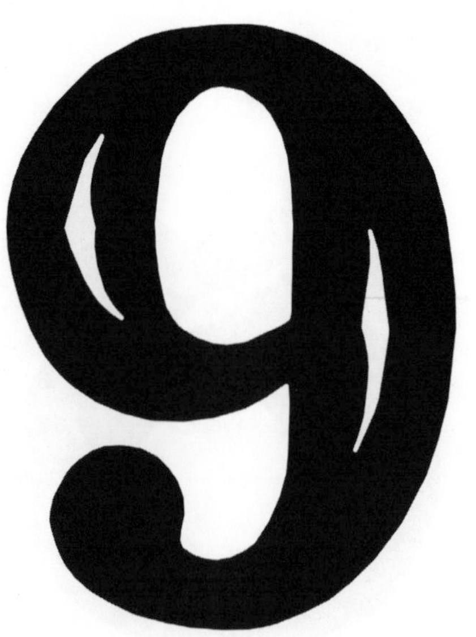

GOOD BYE

YES

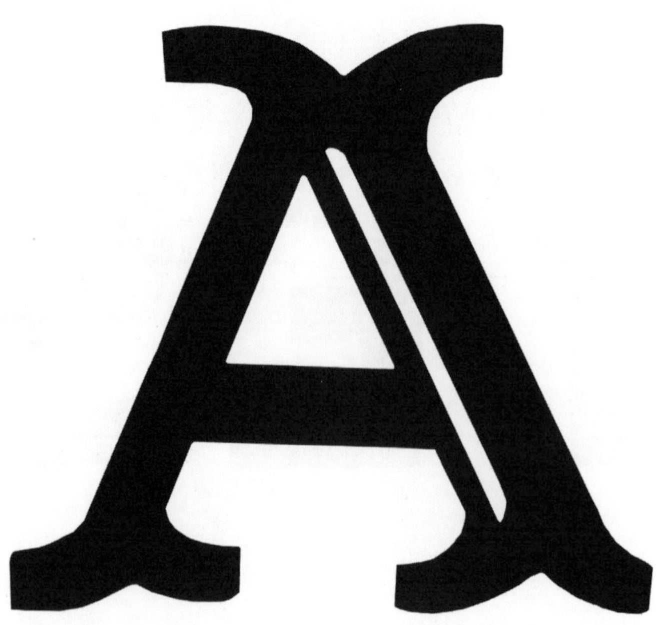

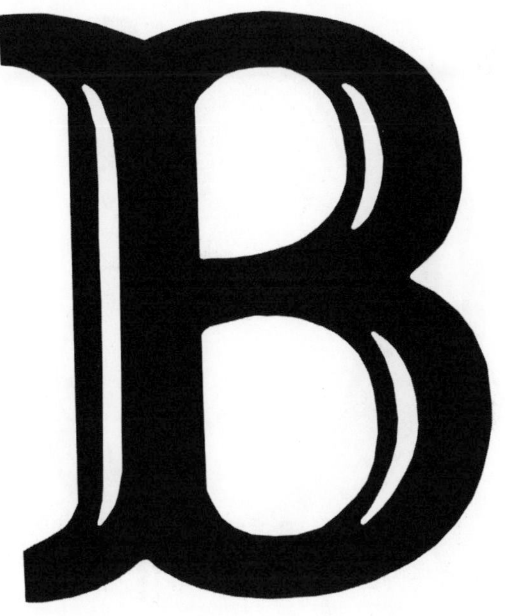

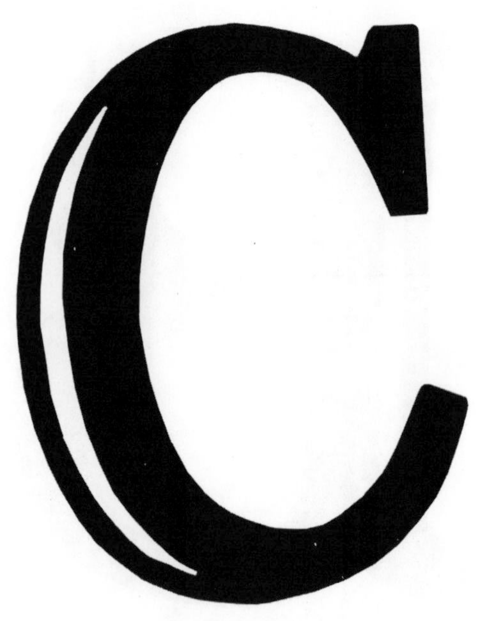

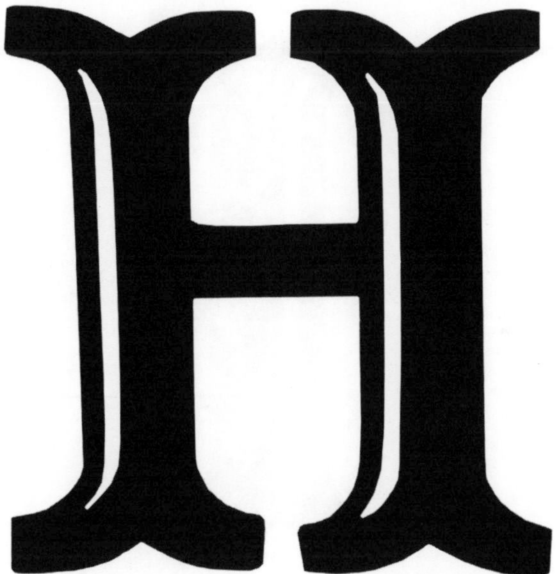

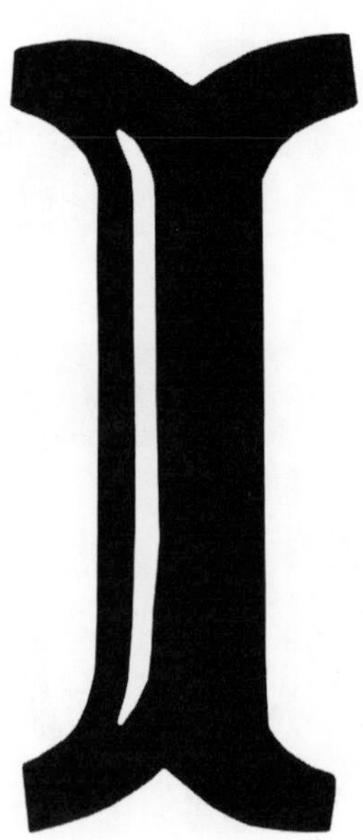

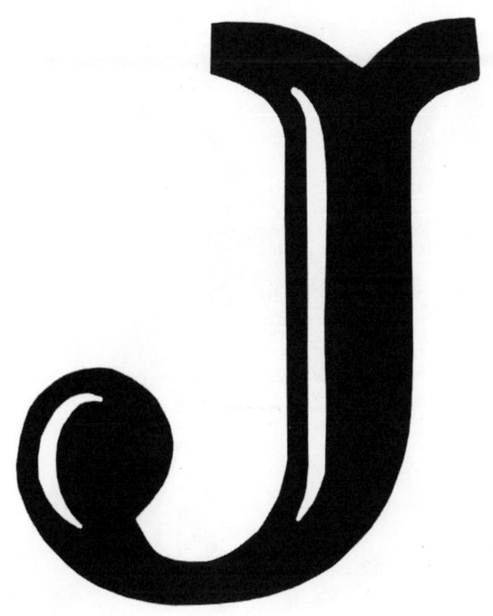

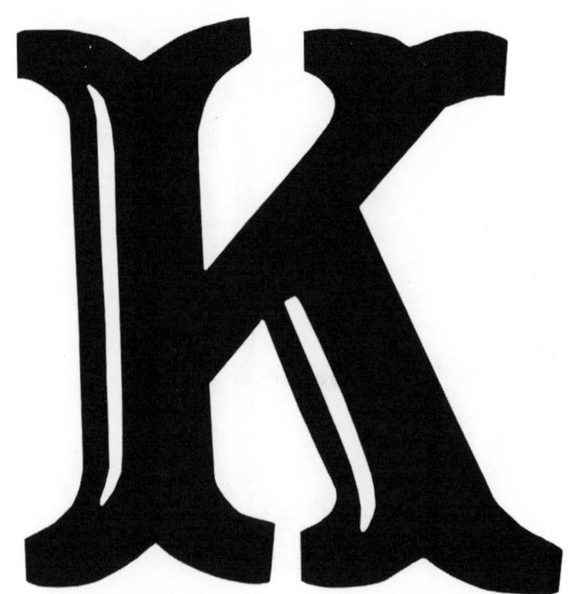

M

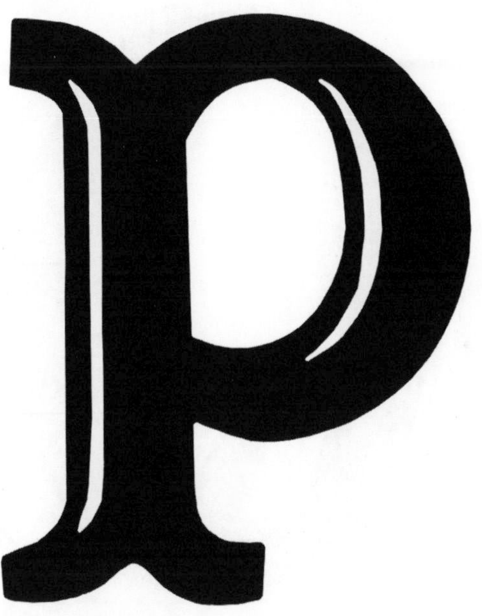

Q

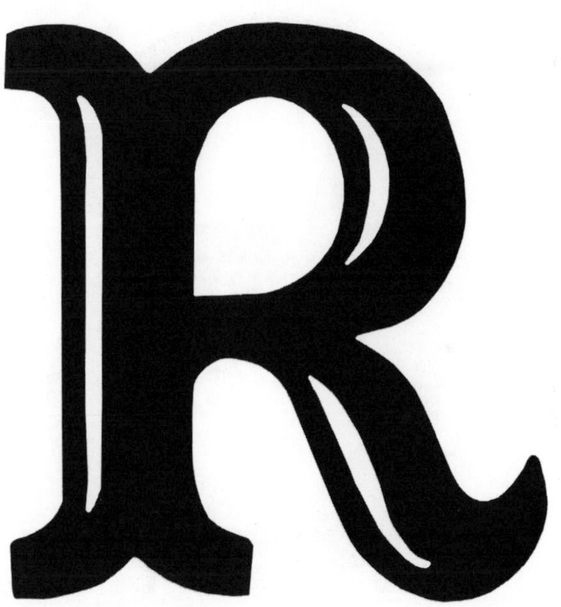

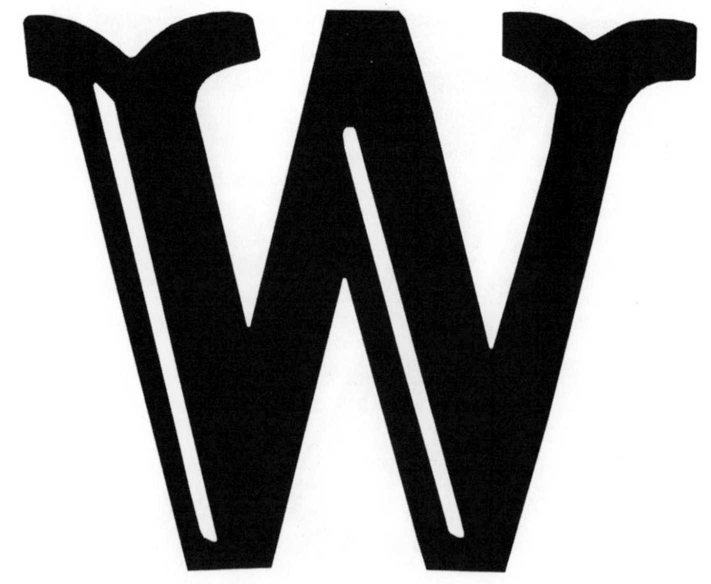

Y

NO

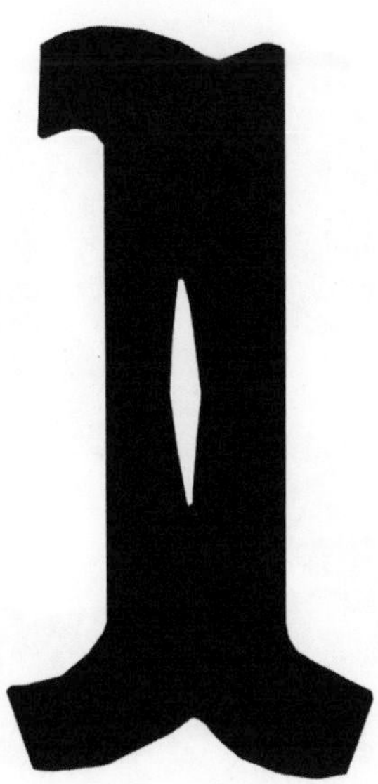

5

GOOD BYE

YES

A

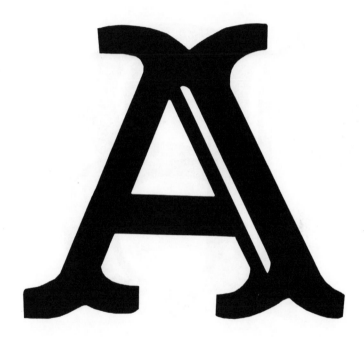

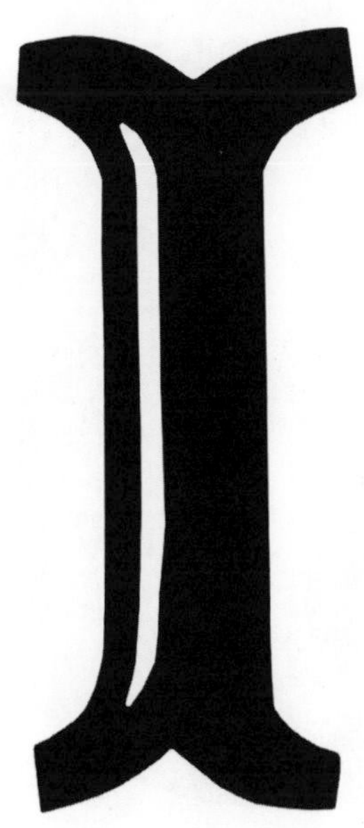

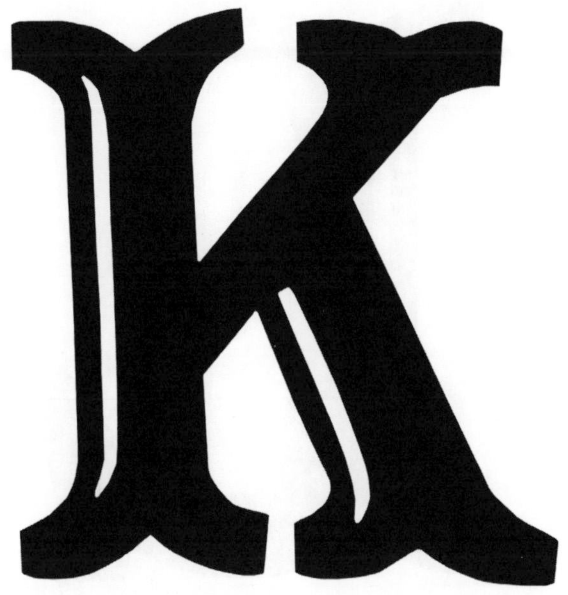

M

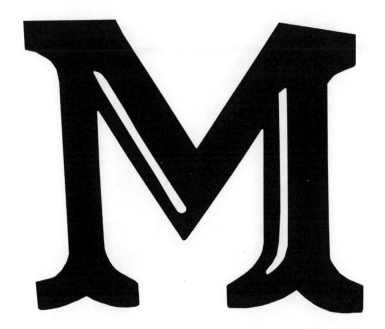

Q

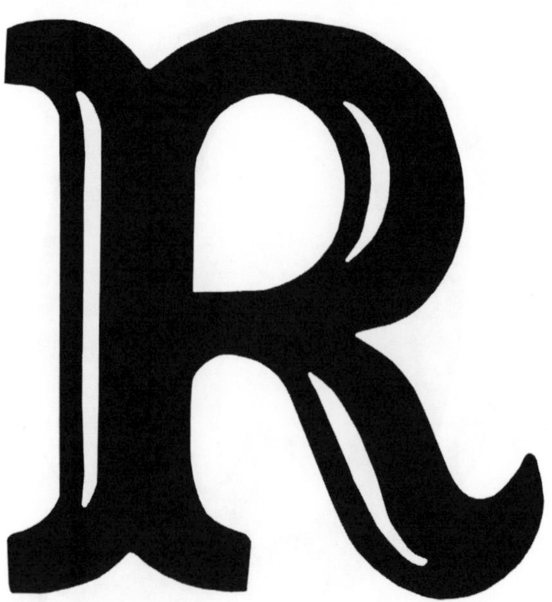

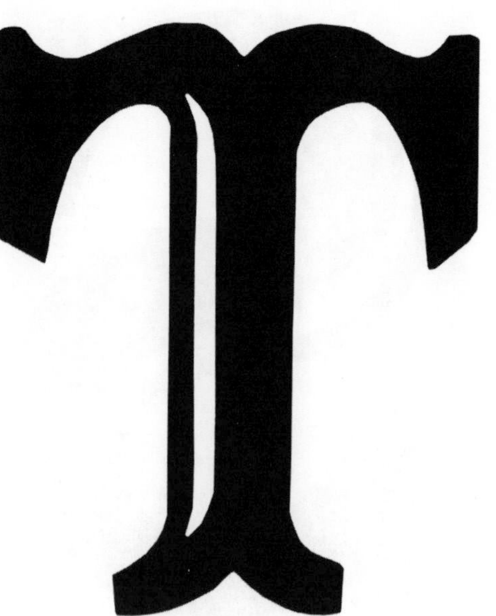

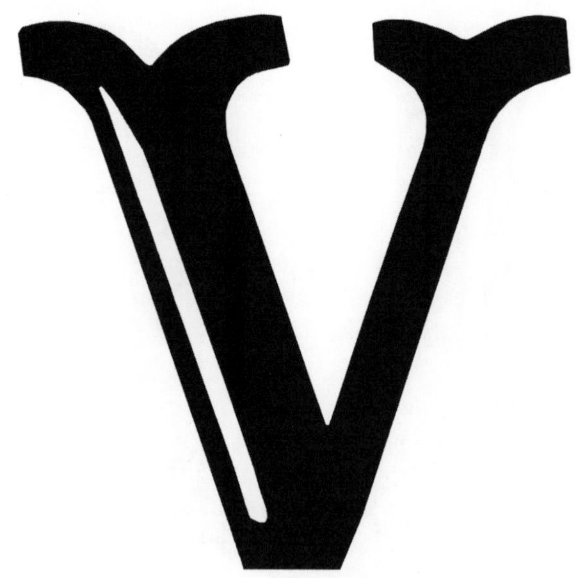

W

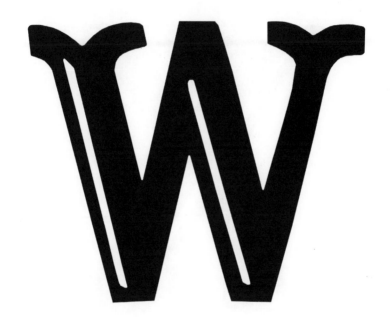

Y

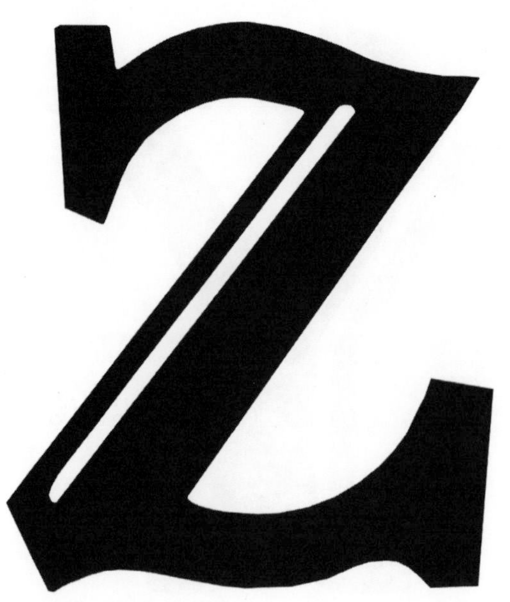

NO

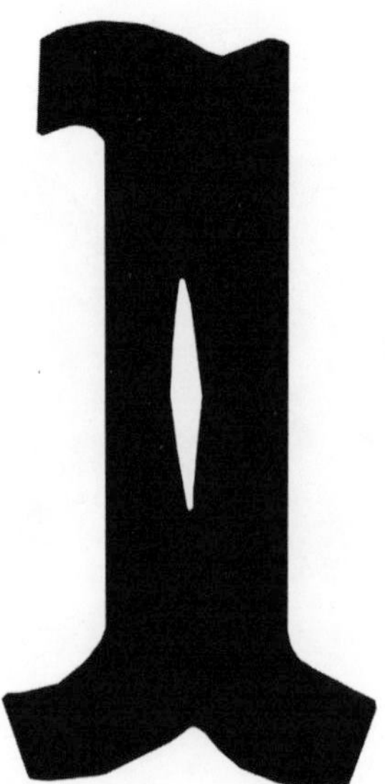

5

GOOD BYE

YES

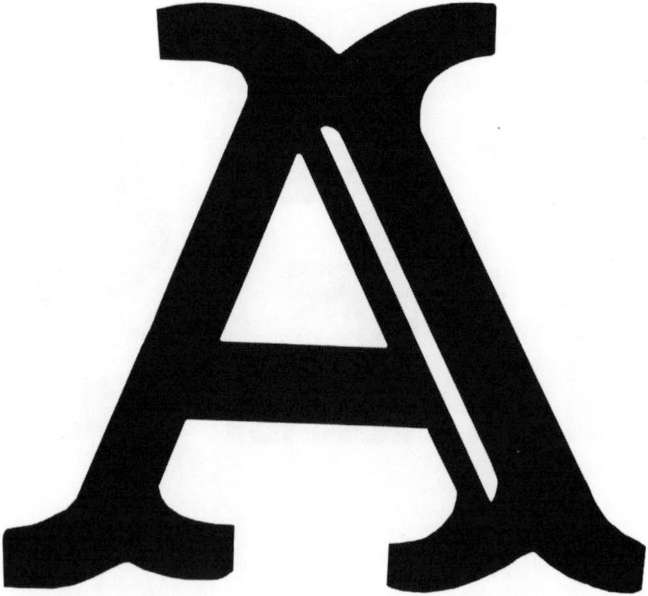

A

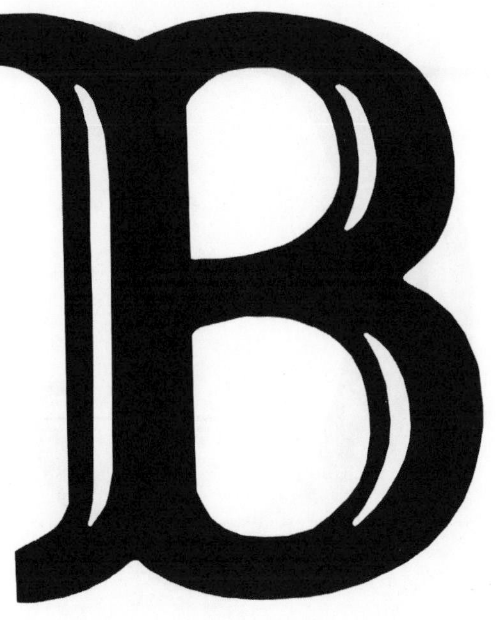

H

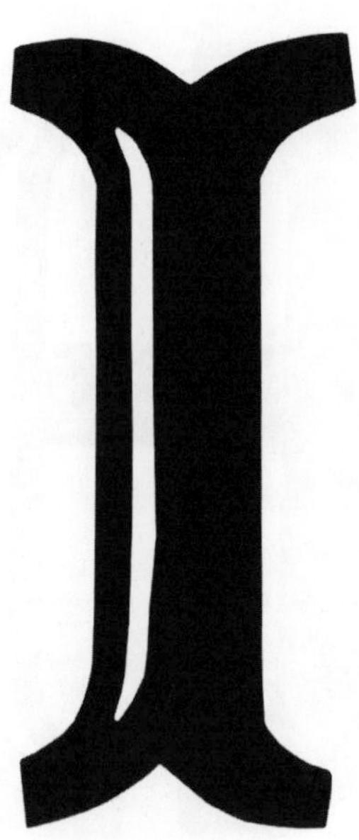

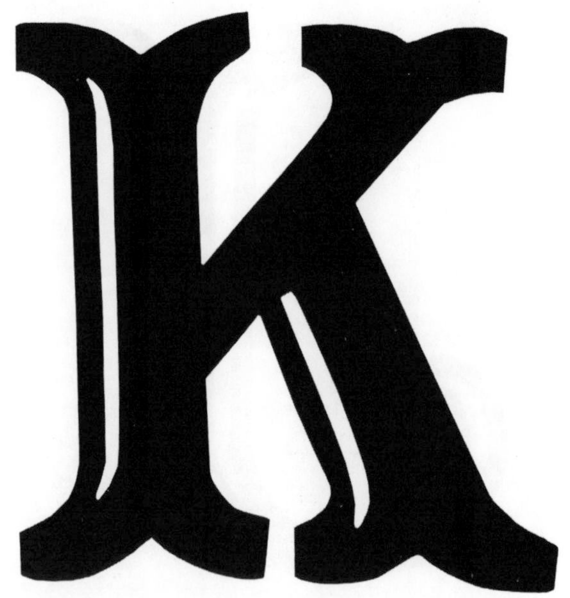

Q

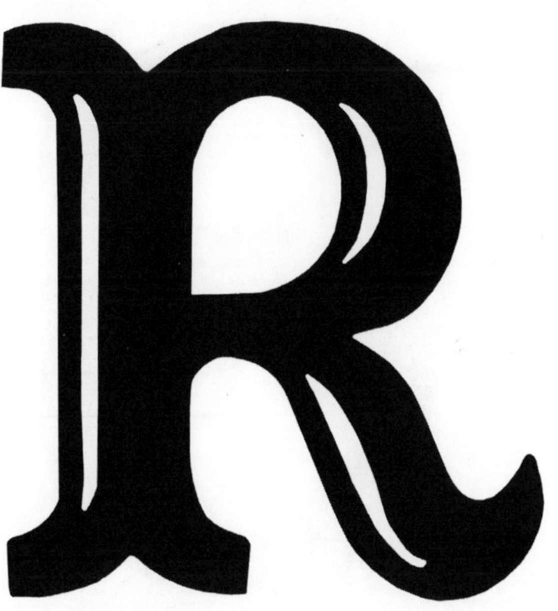

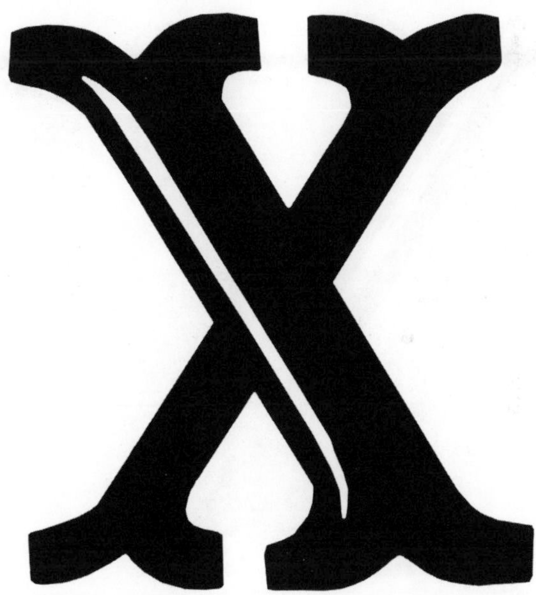

Y

NO

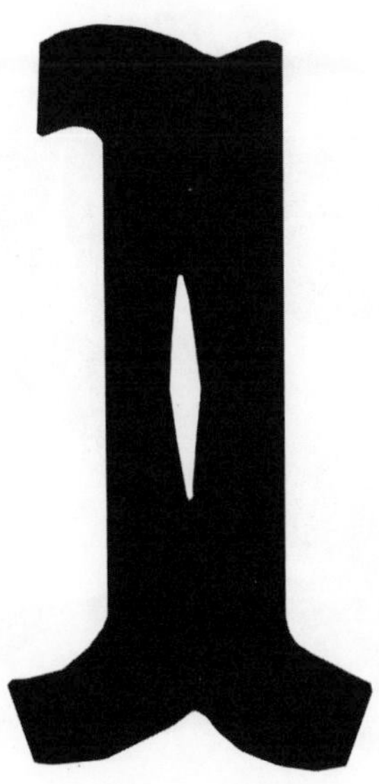

5

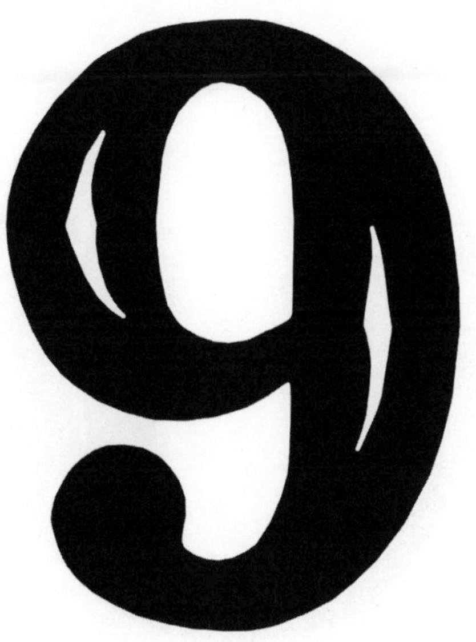

GOOD BYE

YES

A

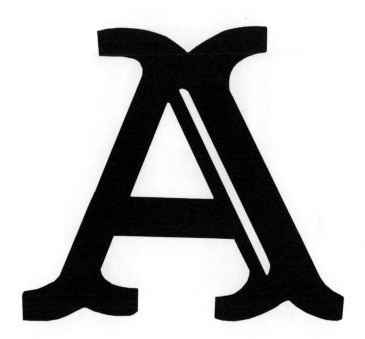

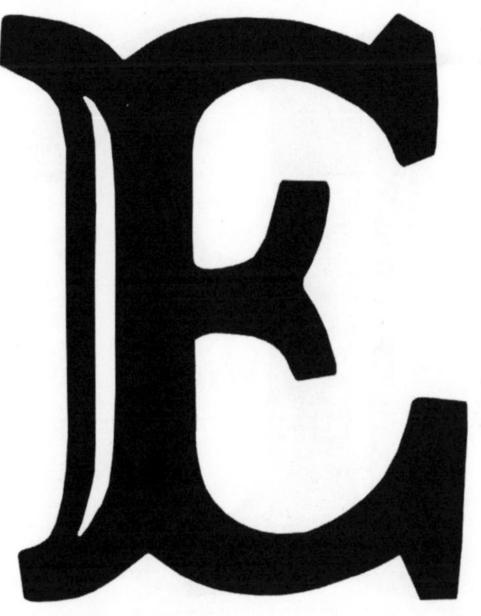

H

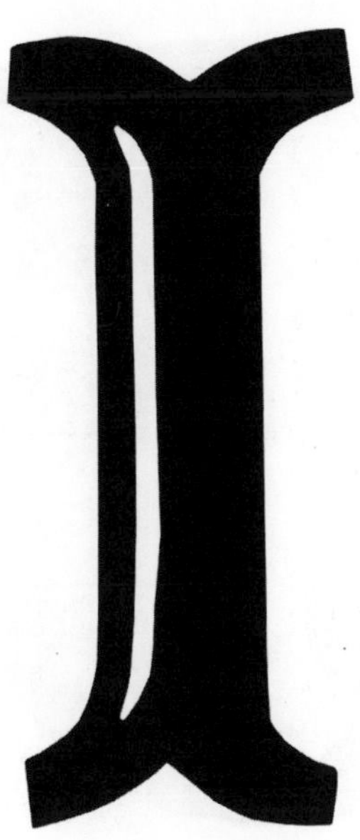

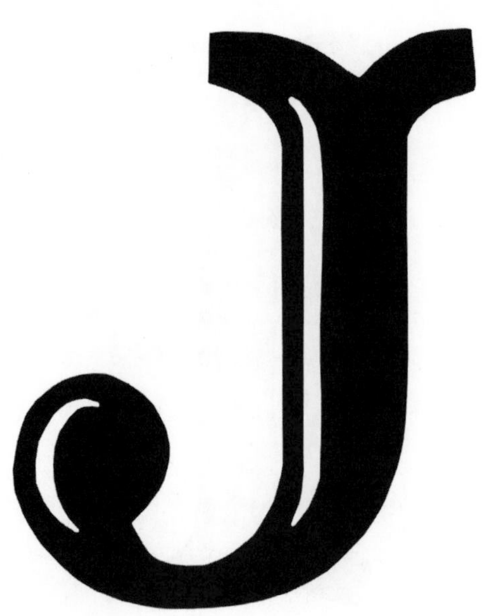

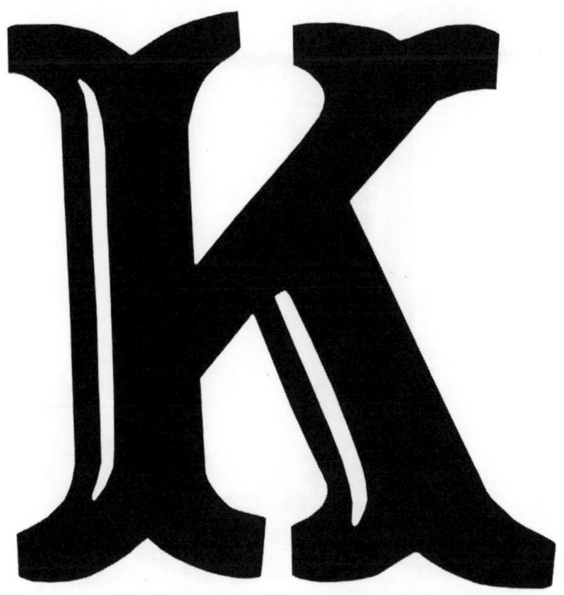

M

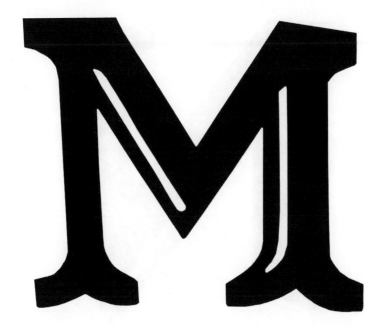

Q

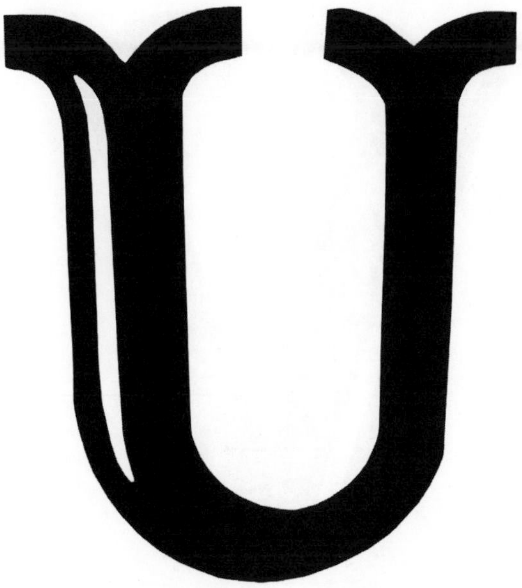

W

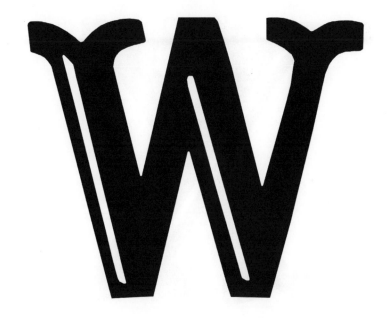

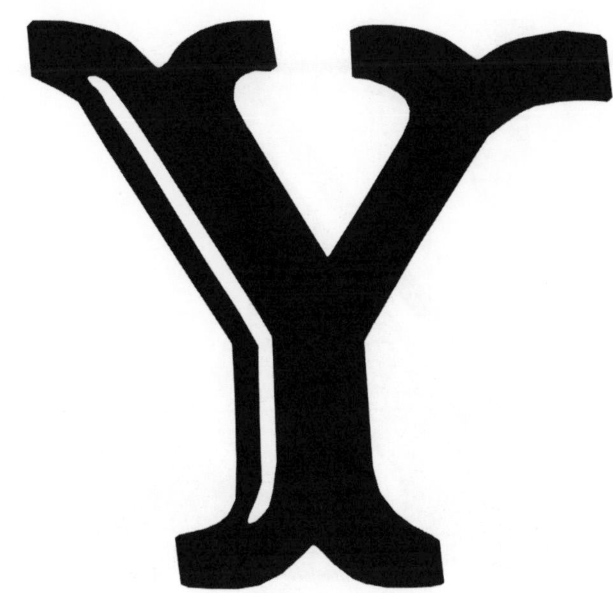

NO

GOOD BYE

YES

A

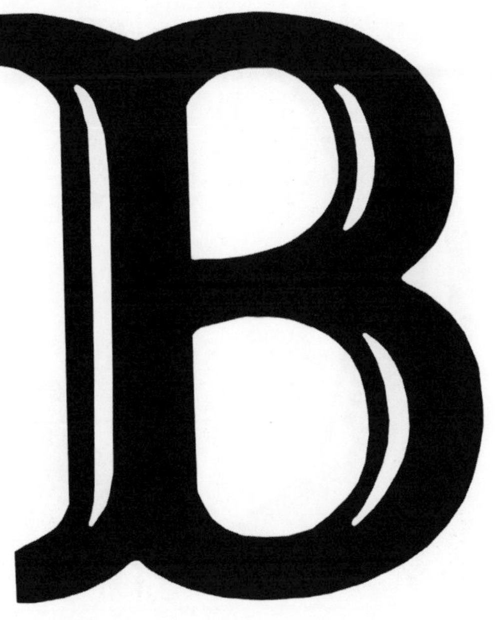

H

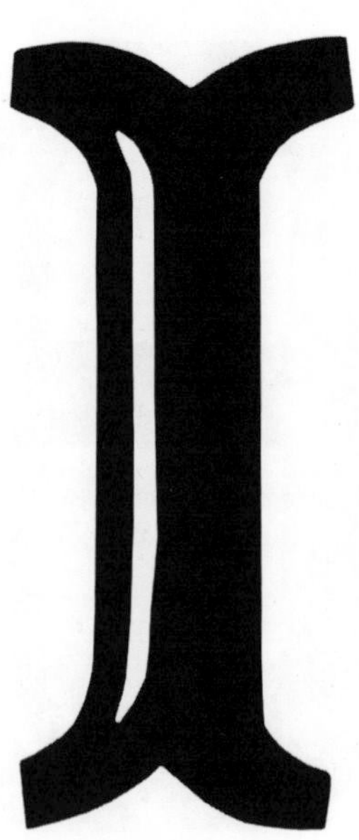

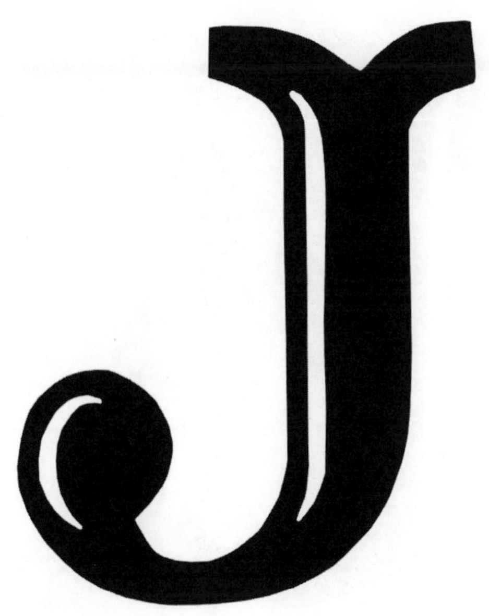

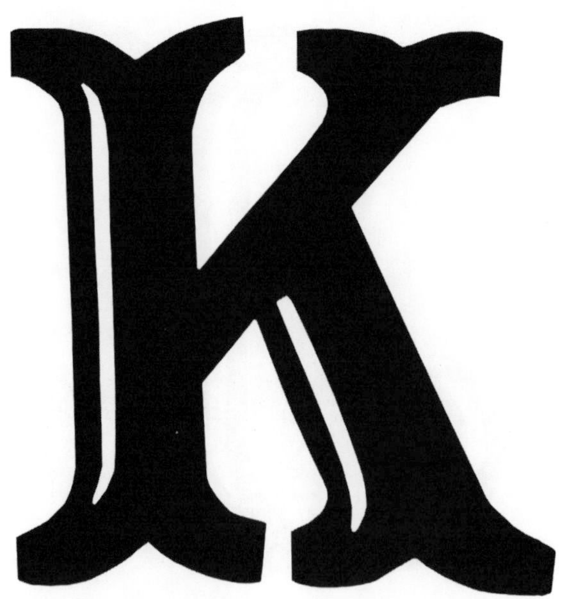

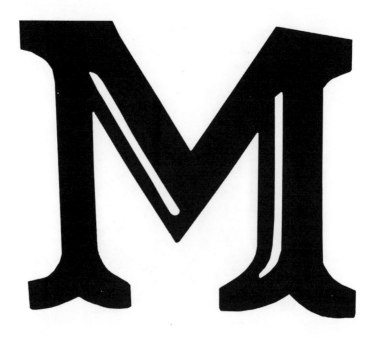

Q

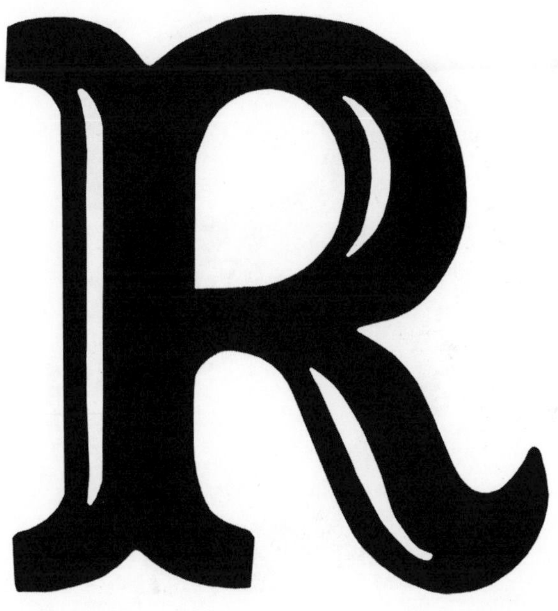

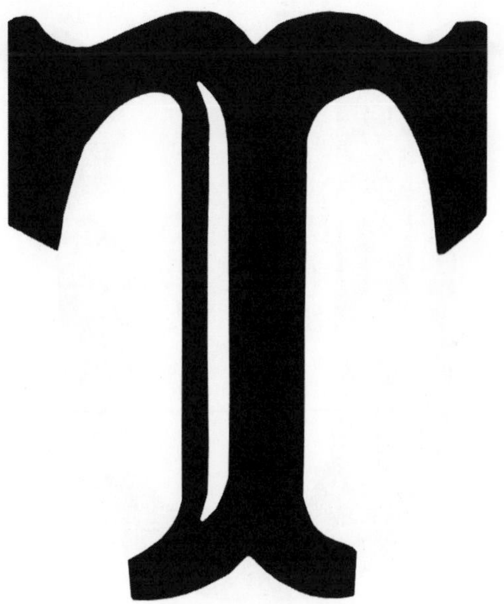

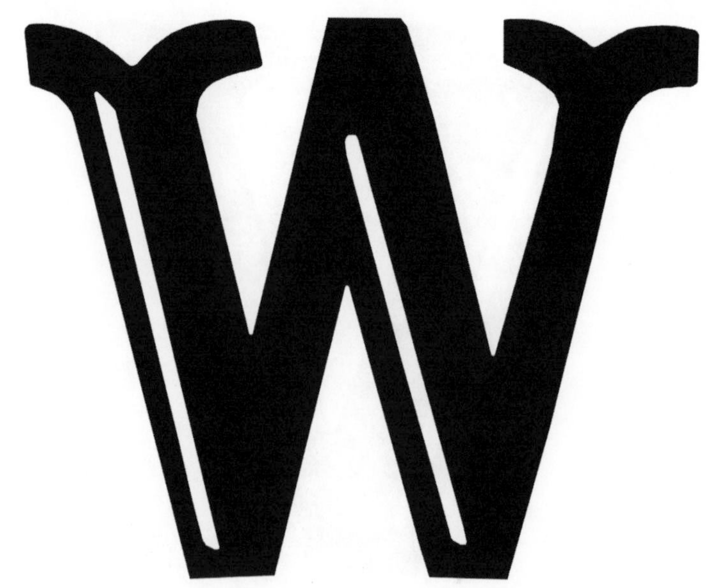

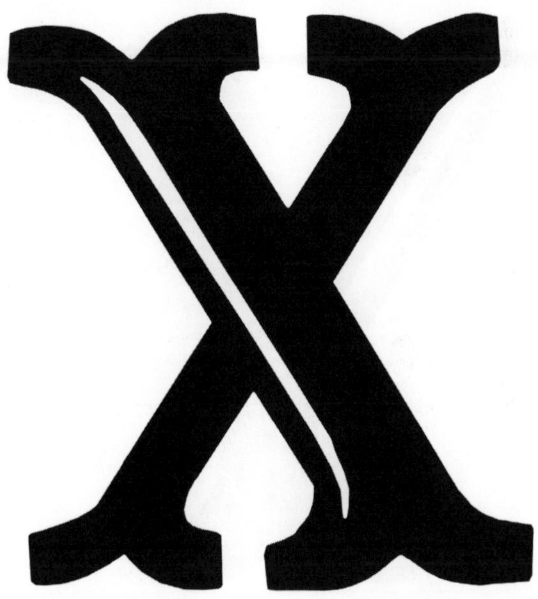

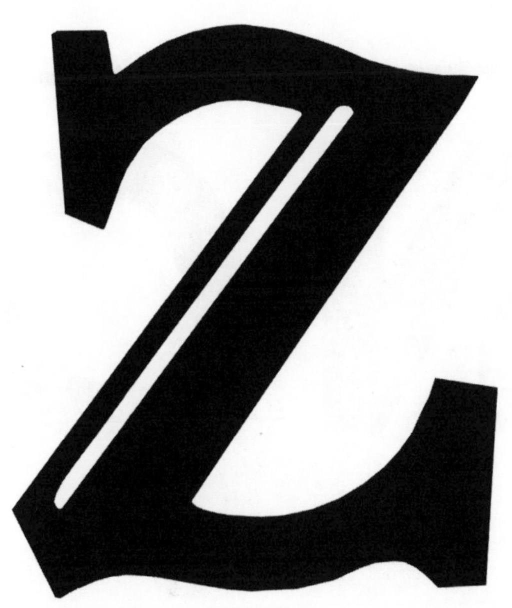

NO

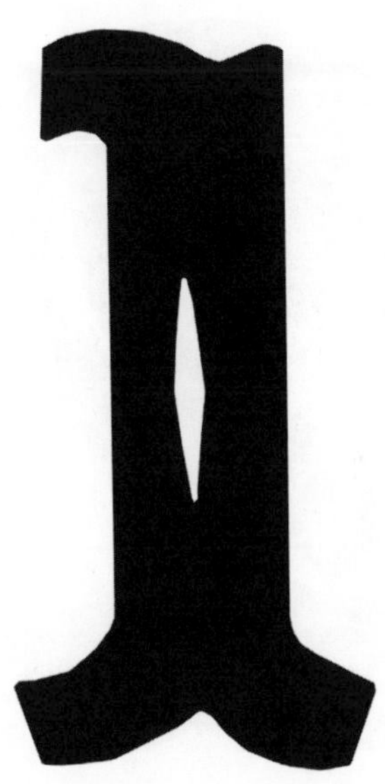

GOOD BYE

YES

A

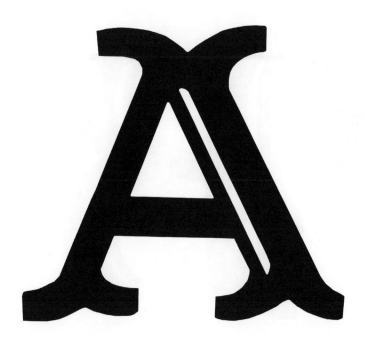

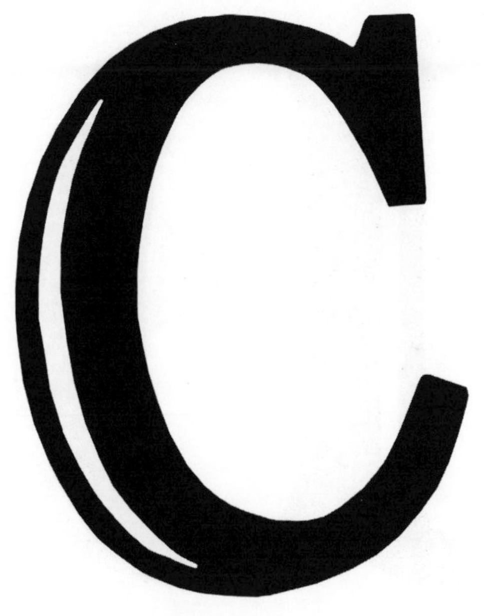

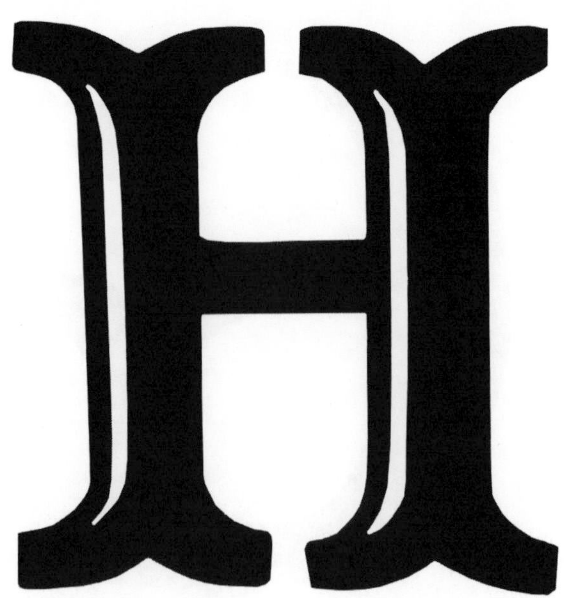

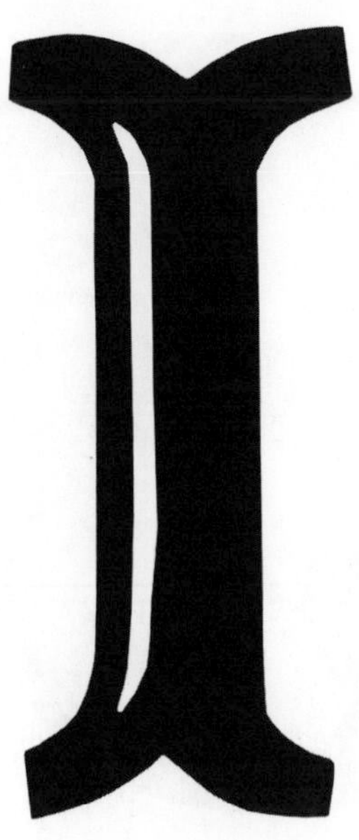

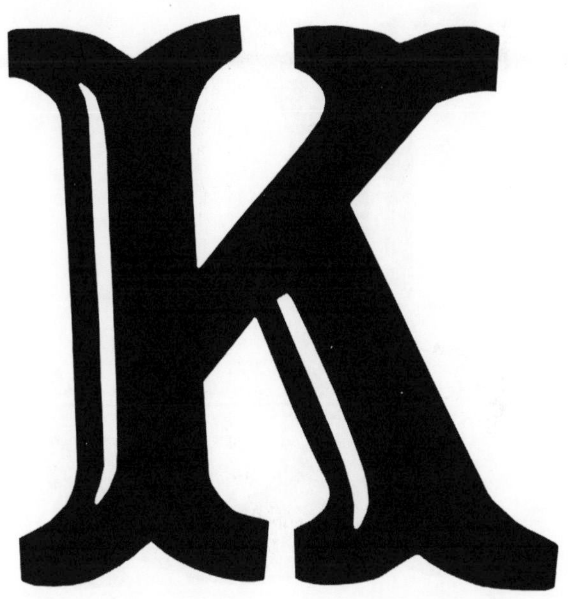

M

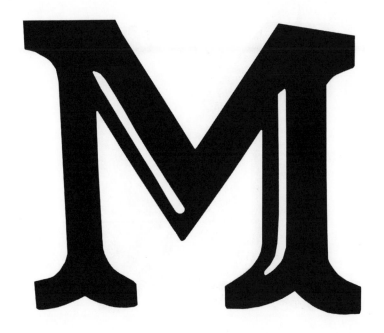

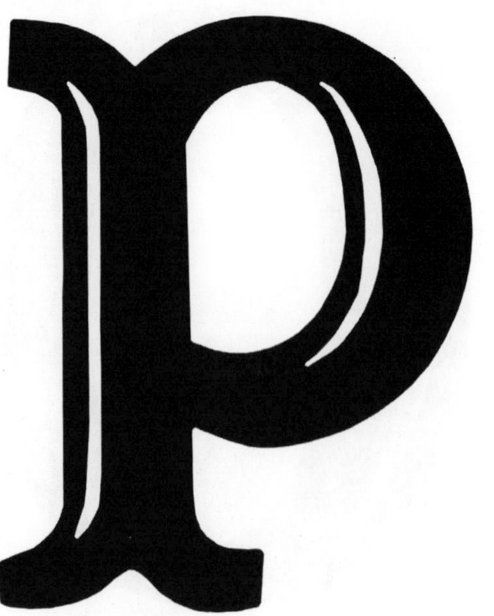

Q

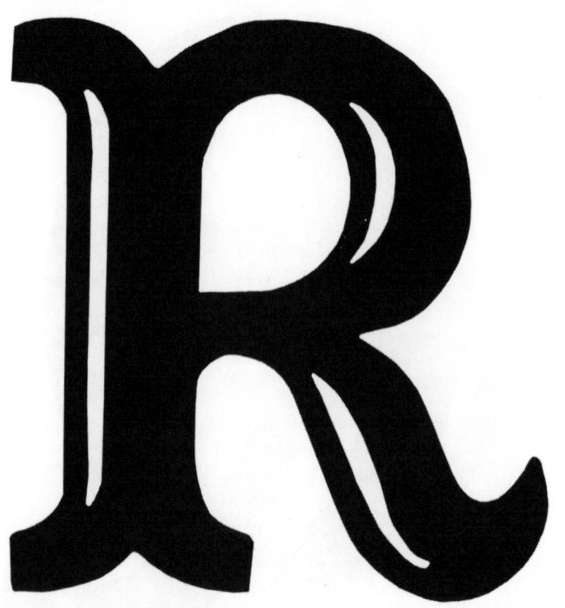

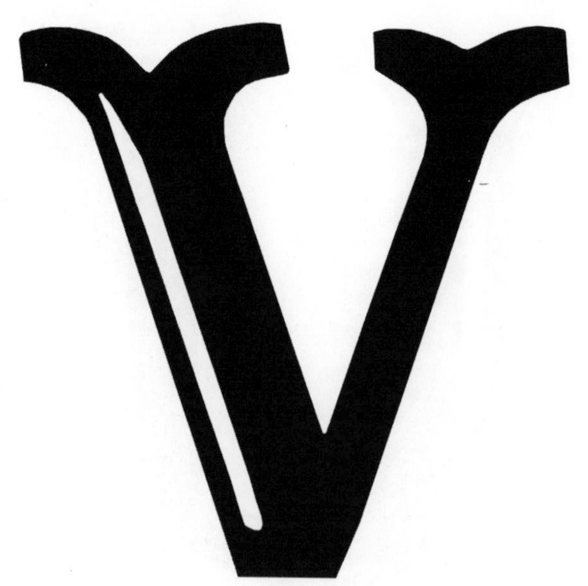

W

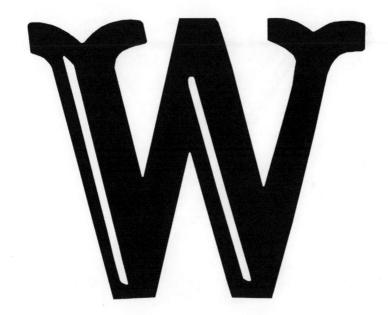

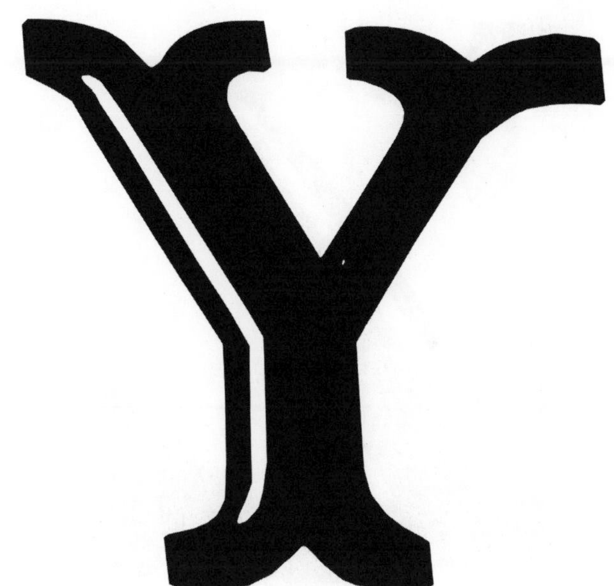

NO

GOOD BYE

YES

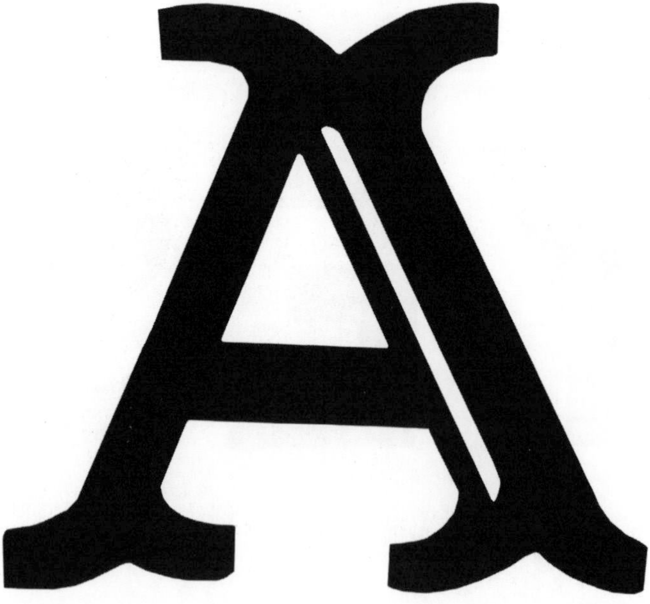

A

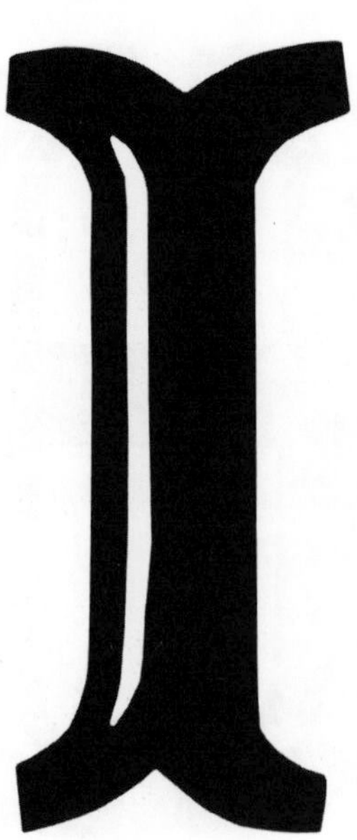

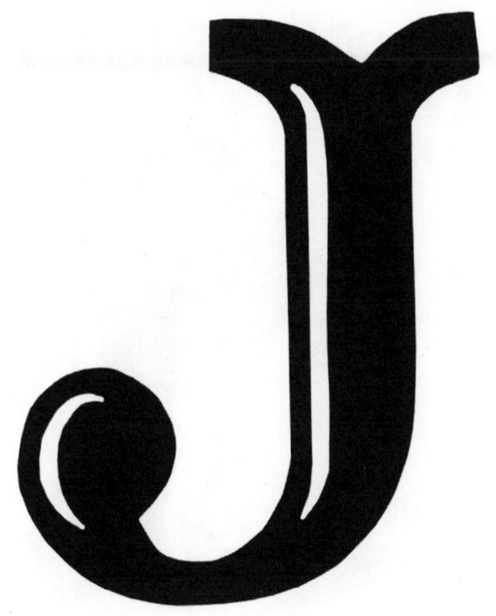

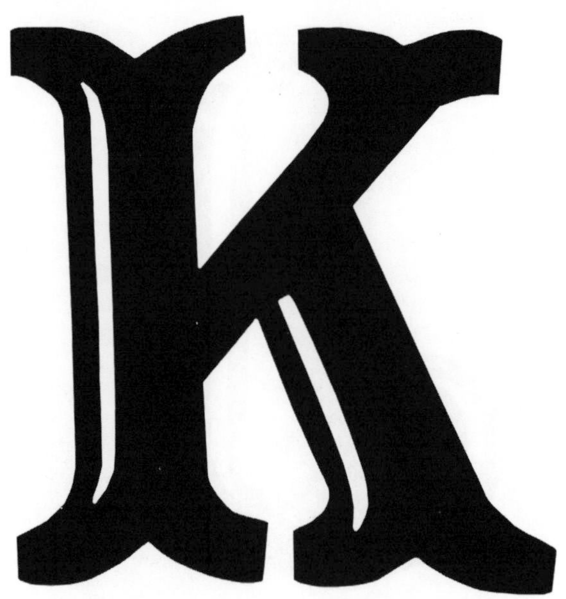

M

Q

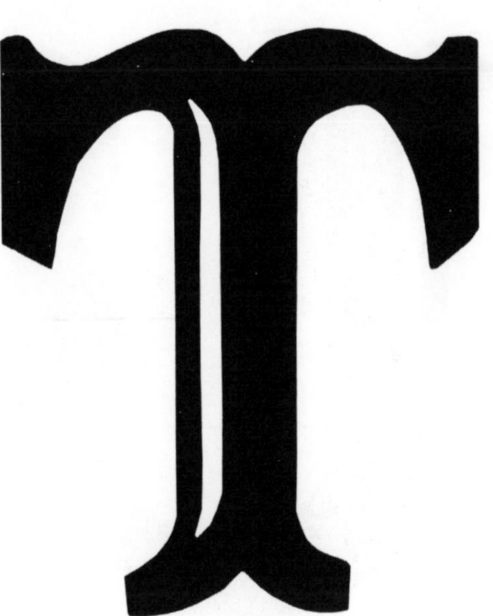

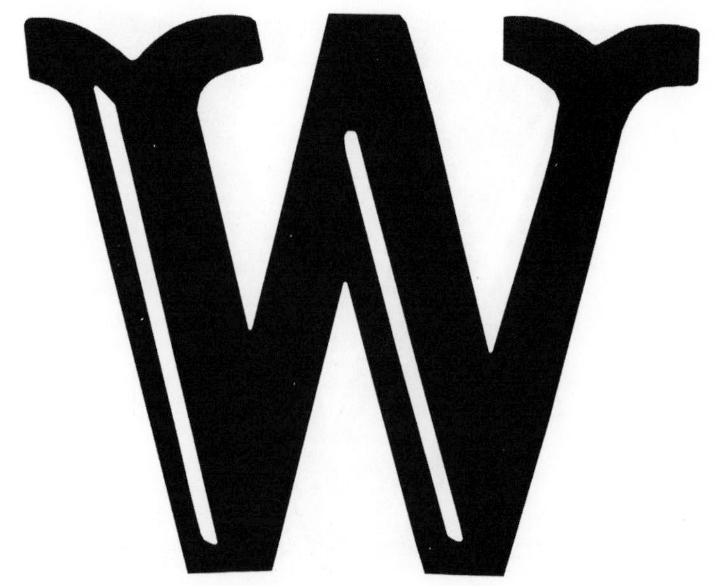

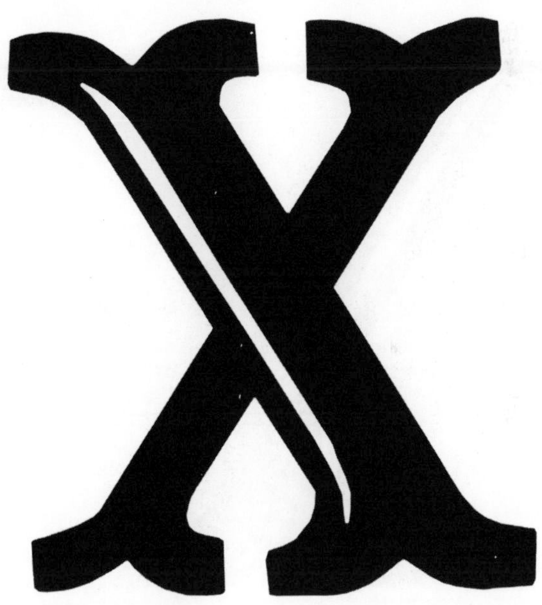

NO

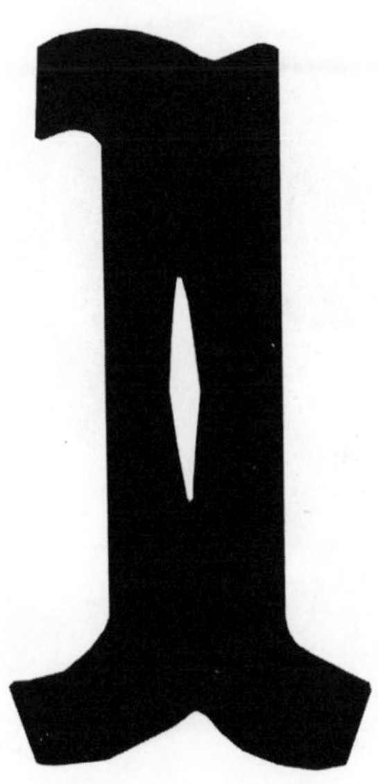

5

GOOD BYE

YES

A

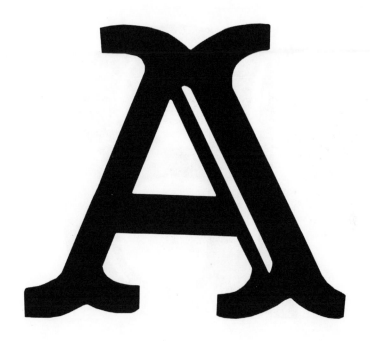

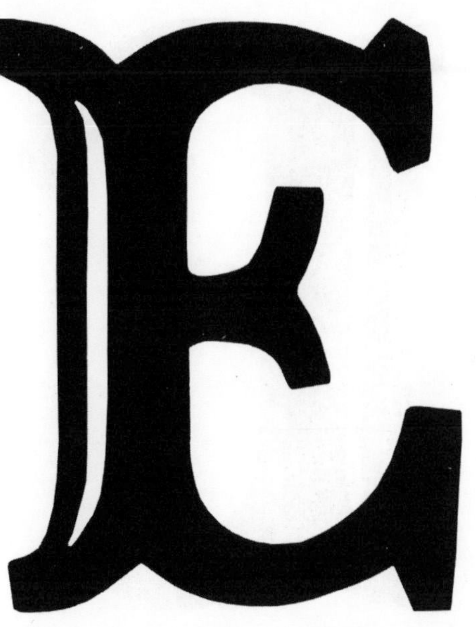

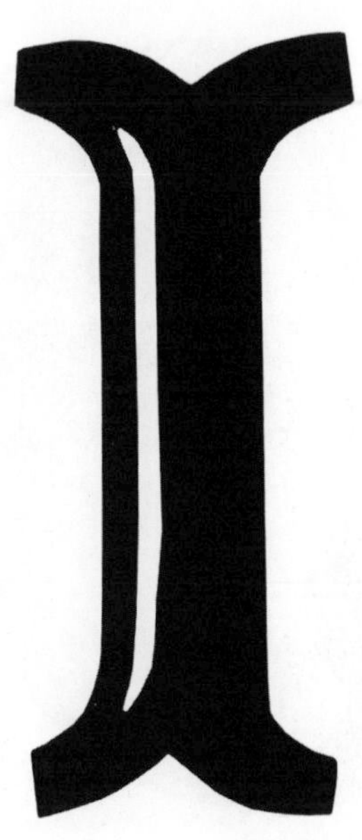

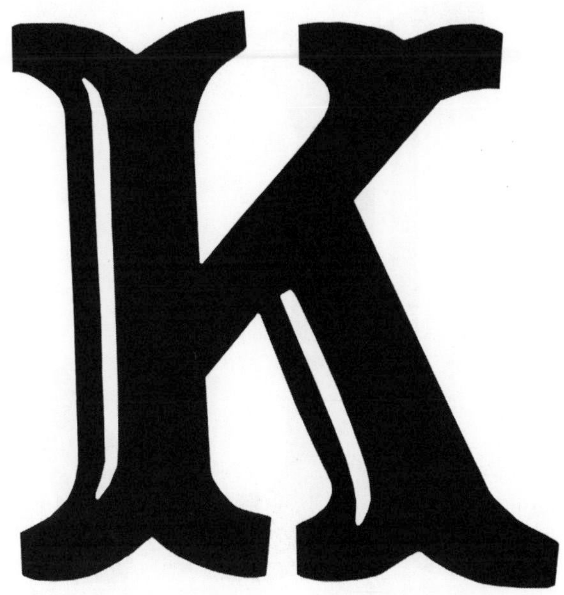

M

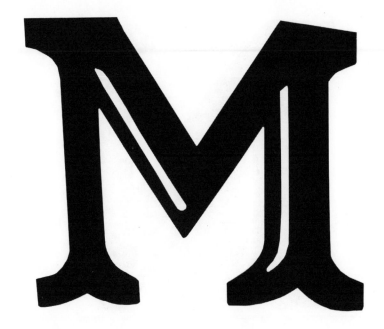

Q

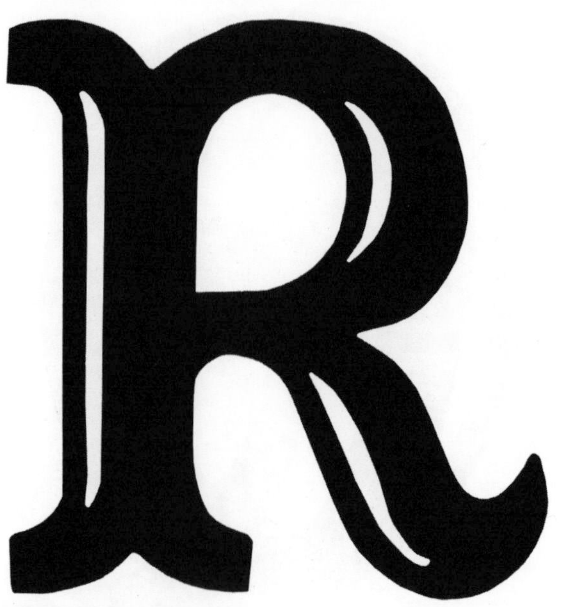

T

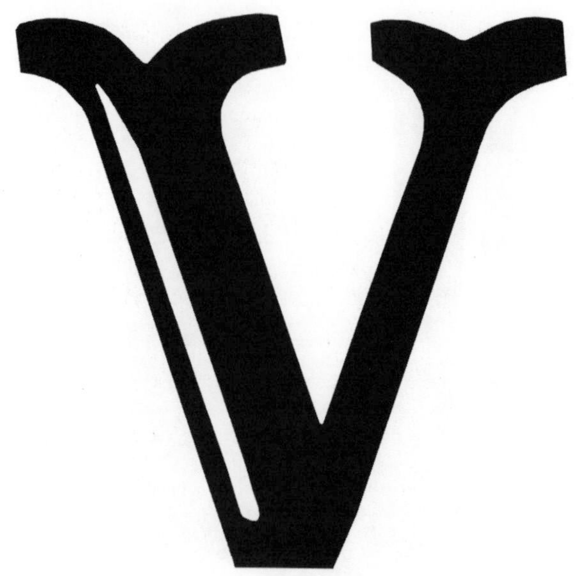

W

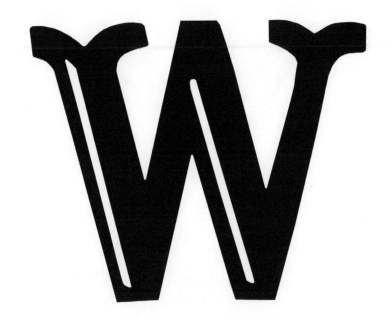

Y

NO

5

GOOD BYE

YES

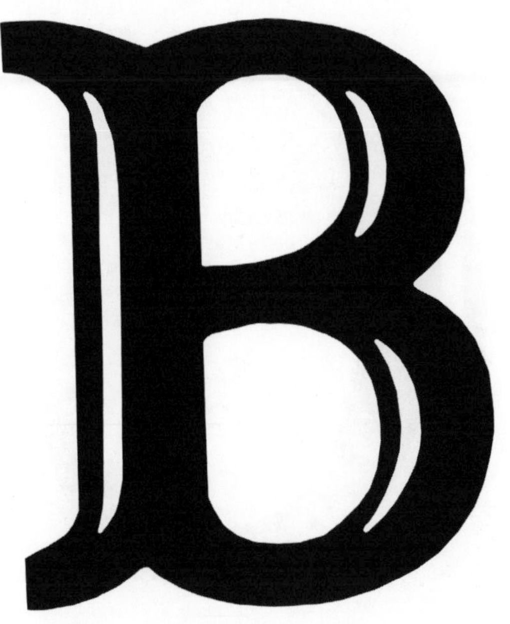

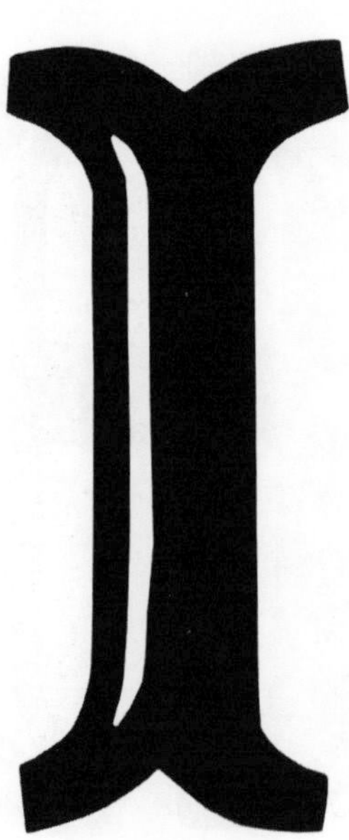

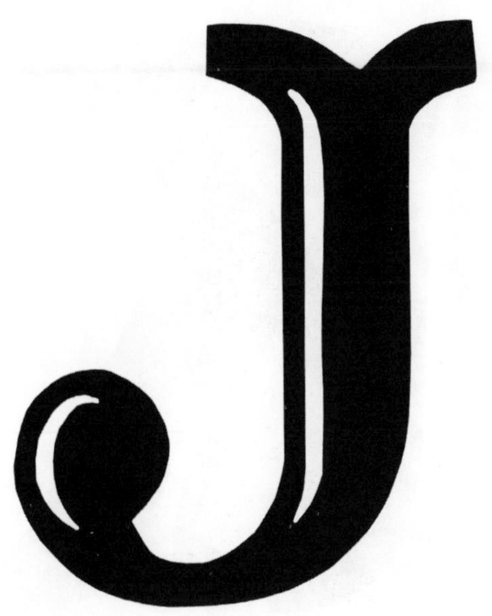

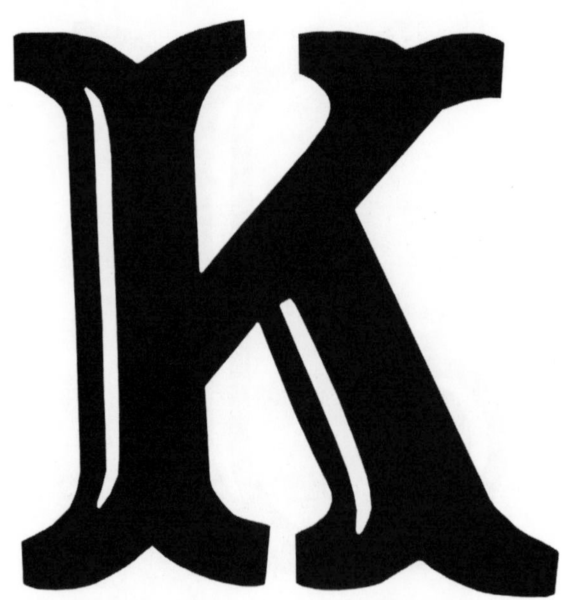

M

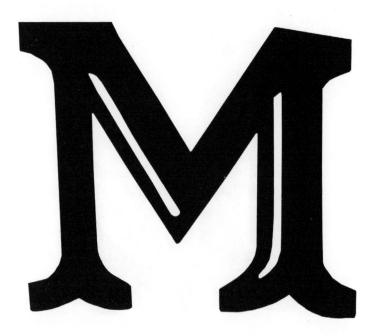

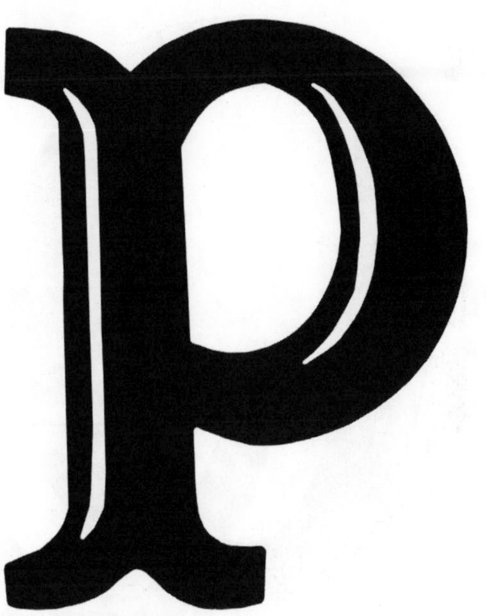

Q

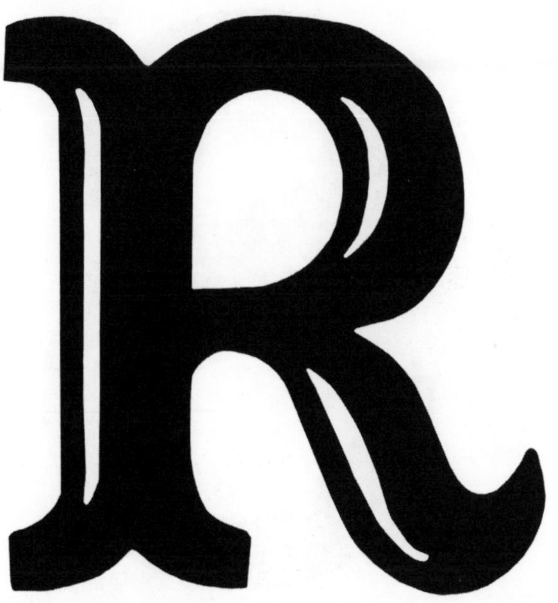

W

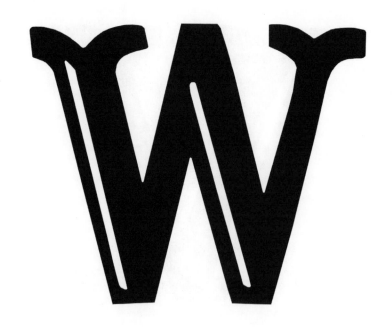

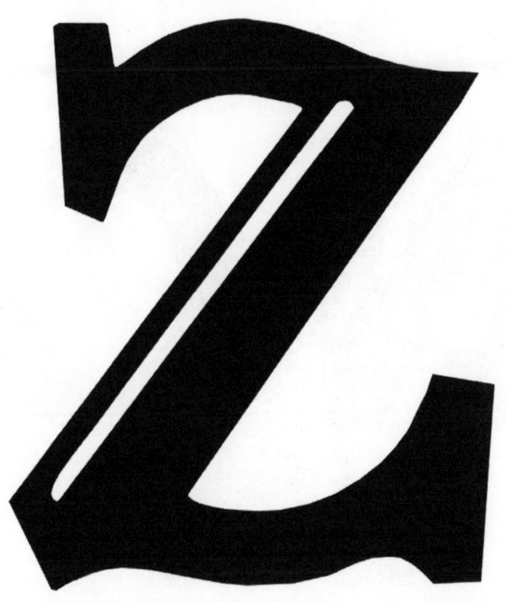

NO

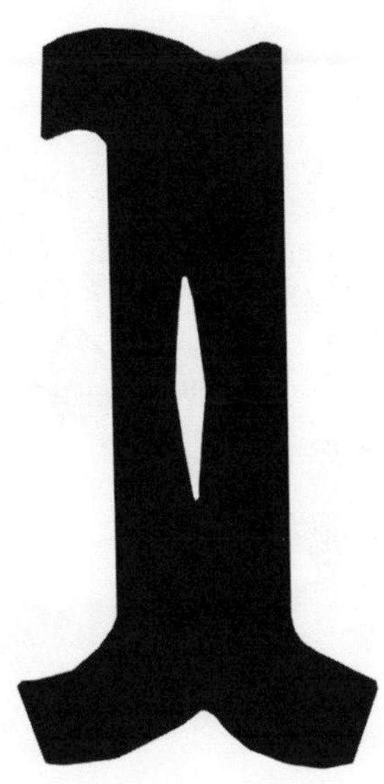

4

GOOD BYE

YES

A

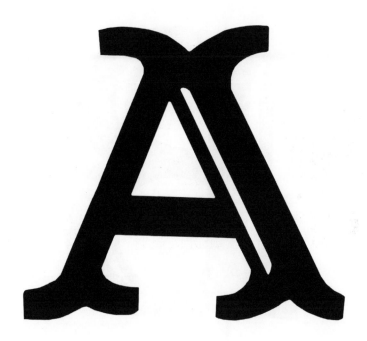

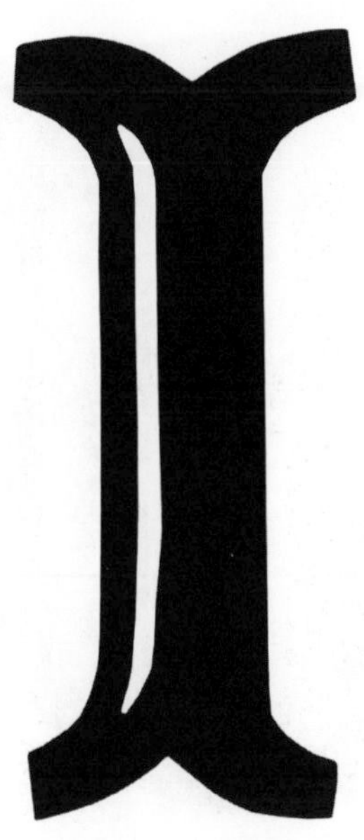

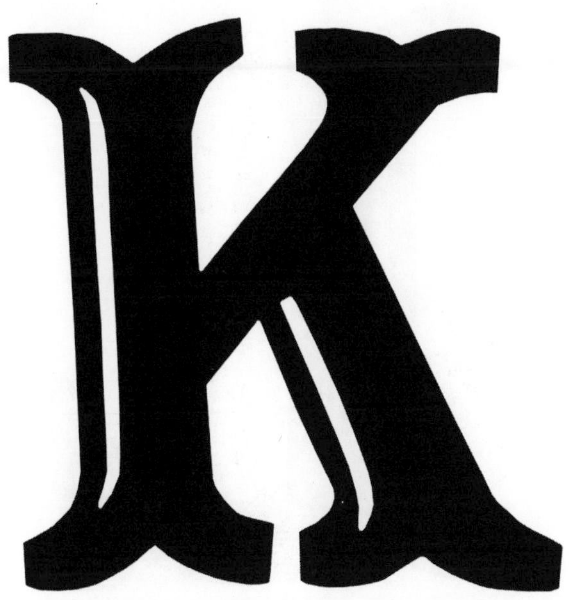

M

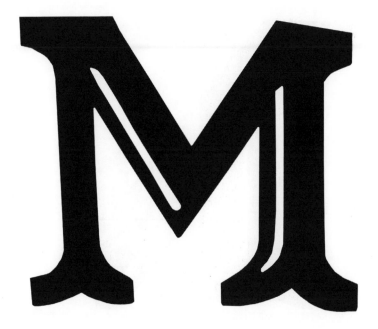

Q

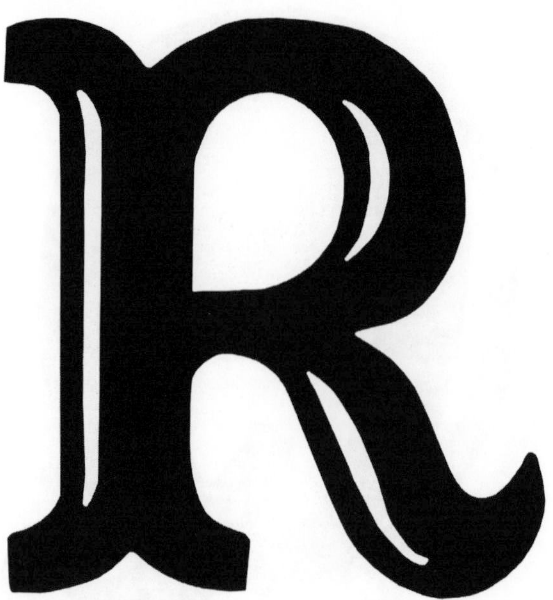

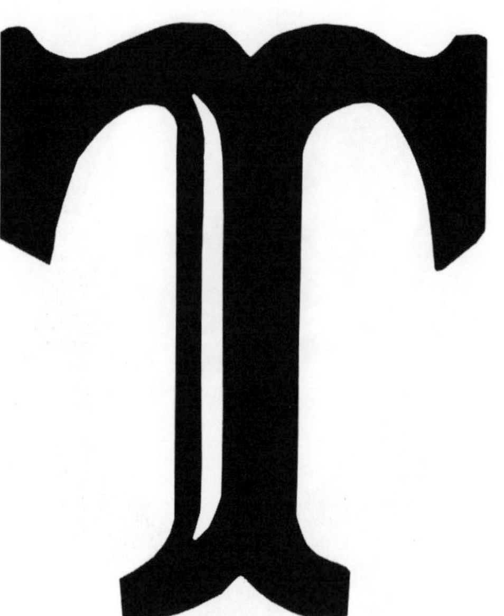

W

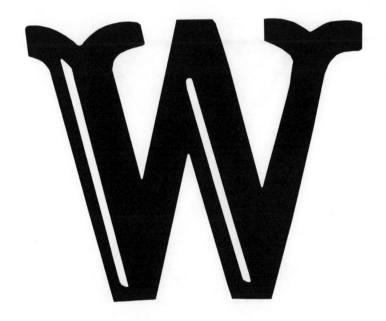

Y

NO

3

5

GOOD BYE

YES

A

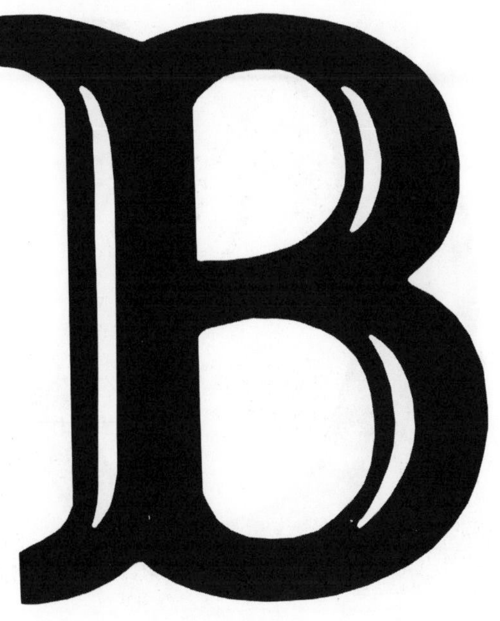

H

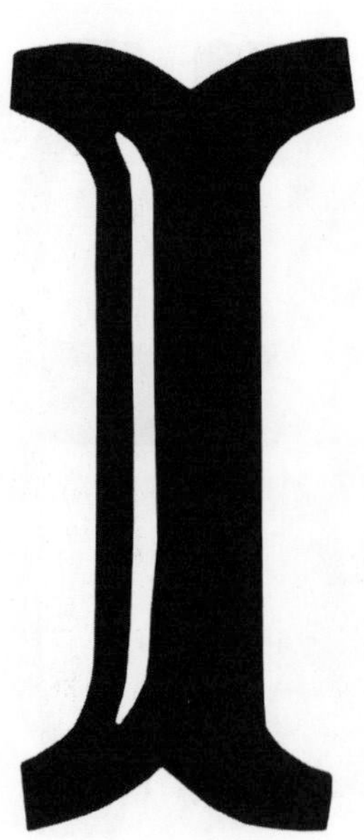

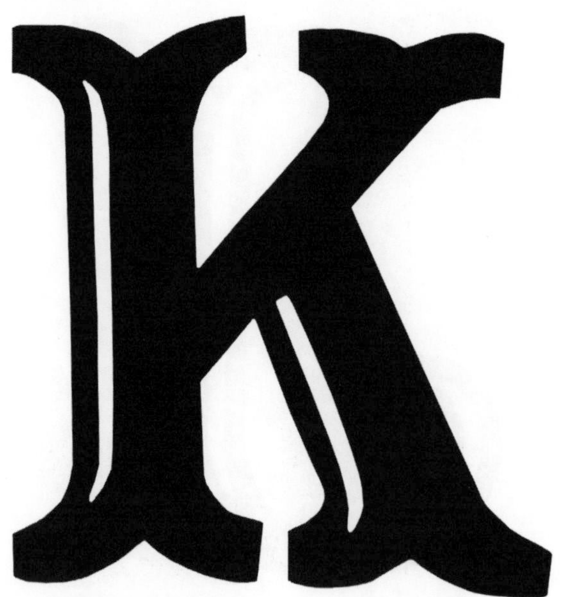

M

Q

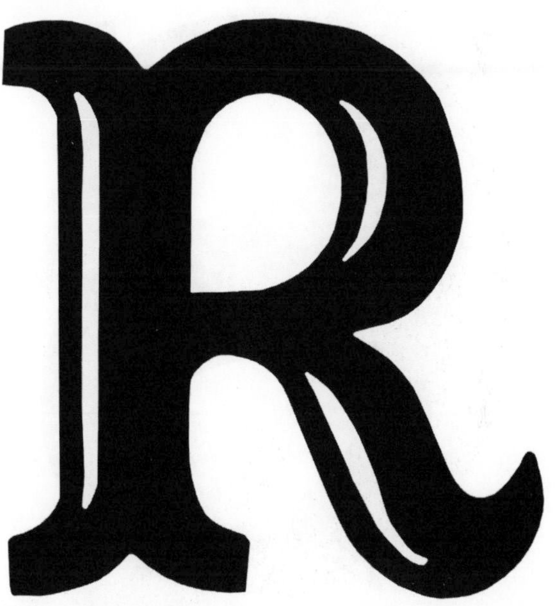

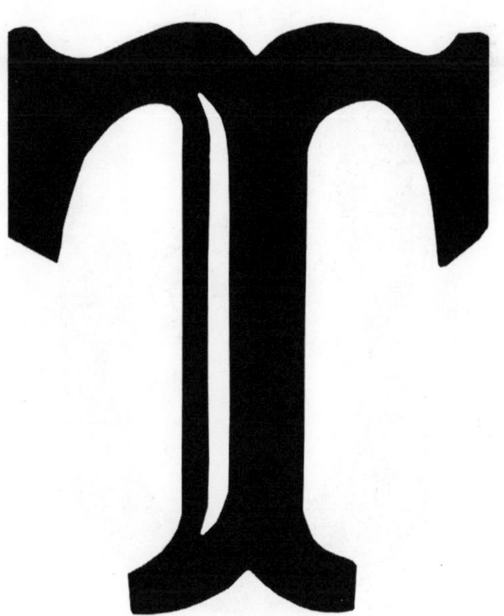

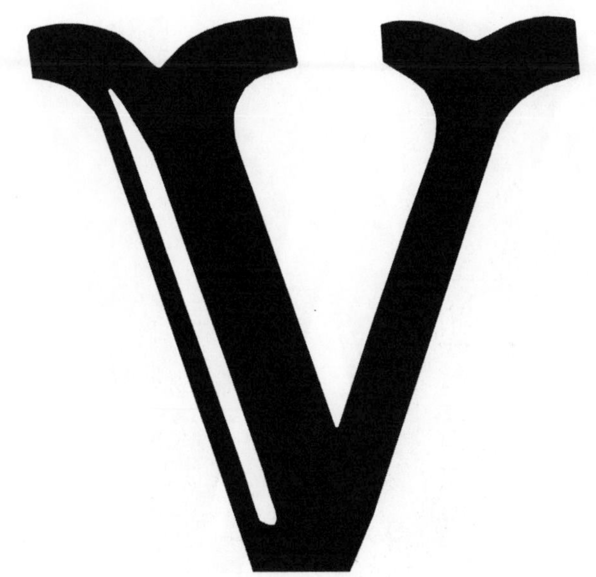

W

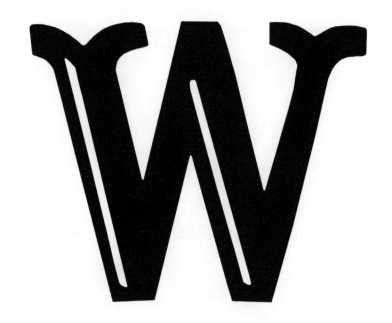

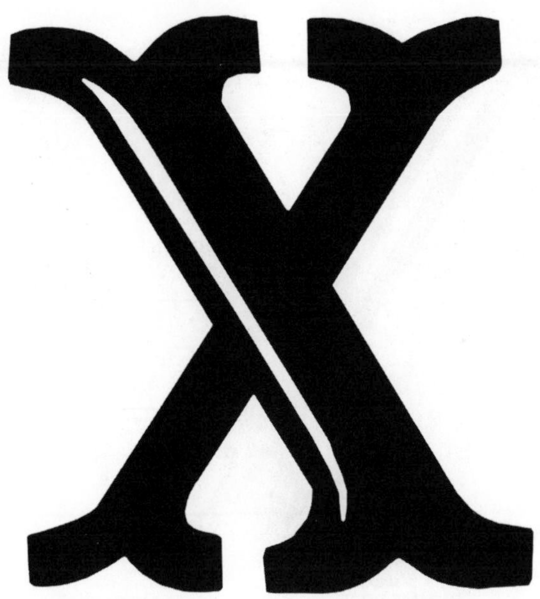

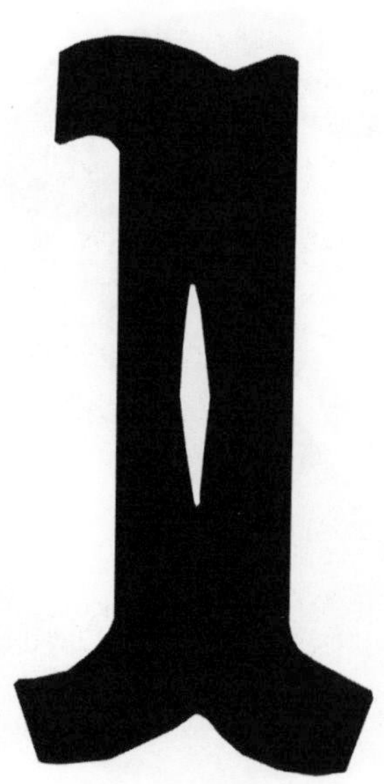

5